From DANIEL McNAIR to US

A history based genealogy of some of
Daniel's descendants with allied lines

Roger B. McNair

The family motto   Work Conquers All
With permission from Andrea Osti on Flikr

I have no doubt at all the Devil grins,
As seas of ink I spatter;
Ye Gods, forgive my "literary" sins,
The other kind don't matter.
From *Rhymes of a Rolling Stone*
Robert Service 1912

From Daniel McNair to Us

Copyright © 2015 by Roger B. McNair

ISBN-13: 978-1519642639

ISBN-10: 1519642636

Dedicated to my brothers Norman David McNair,
John Rupert McNair, Doyle Brian McNair,
and Michael Price McNair,

.

.

.

.

and of course,
our young 'uns,

.

.

.

and theirs,

.

.

.

and theirs...

**Dedicated to my brothers Norman David McNair,
John Rupert McNair, Doyle Brian McNair,
and Michael Price McNair,**

.

.

.

.

**and of course,
our young 'uns,**

.

.

.

and theirs,

.

.

.

and theirs…

Table of Contents

Introduction

On Father's day in 1957, my brother Doyle gave our dad a gift in the form of a book titled *McNair, McNear, and McNeir Genealogies* by James Birtley McNair, copyrighted 1955. About ten years after dad died, my mother passed the book on to me, and I have been keen on it ever since. Tracing the roots, branches, and stumps of the family tree became my hobby and eventually a consuming passion. I began tracing out the lineage for dad, and my mother, Kathryn, and also the mother of my brothers, dad's first wife, Sibyl.

Over the past several years I have made several trips to Salt Lake City, where the Mormon Church makes publicly available to everyone their vast and extensive collections of census records, tax and land records, and thousands of books and other records in their genealogical library, and have made other trips to more direct sources of information in Pennsylvania, Tennessee, and North Carolina. I was enthralled with every precious bit of data garnered from county records, local historians, genealogical societies and libraries, and from inscriptions on tombstones. I dutifully recorded it all on 3x5 cards, then on charts called pedigrees and family group sheets, and eventually recorded it in genealogical software. I was researching every related surname, every marriage, birth, death, in-law, out-law, and cousin, whether first or second, even twice or thrice removed. By golly, I was getting it all down. Unfortunately, what I ended up with was just data; over 650 marriages and the names of over 3,300 individuals, but with no story to tell, and no real sense of our history. These records were just fossils in our geologic ancestry, buried in the stratum of time.

That realization compelled me to shift the focus of my research from raw data collection to flesh and blood ancestry study. Who were these people in my computer? What were they thinking and doing? When did they live, in a historical context? Where were they living and where were they moving to? Why did they blaze trails, ford rivers, cross mountains, put their families and themselves into difficult situations, often even into grave danger, forge bonds, form alliances, and build a country out of a wilderness? Of course I had tidbits of stories gathered along the way, but not really enough to begin to answer my questions or salve my soul. Thus the emphasis morphed into a quest for people, instead of names. I knew their names, but I did not know them. The time had come to hang some ornaments on the family tree.

The book that Doyle gave to dad is now tattered and worn, dinged on every corner, broken in the spine, losing its cover, and pockmarked with penciling in the margins by myself and my son Shannon. That is to say, well-worn and well loved. That book is 458 pages and covers a wide swath of possible (but not yet connected) cousins and kinfolk, of England, Scotland, Ireland, Canada, New Zealand, Maryland, New York, North Carolina, Pennsylvania, and finally twenty-eight pages on the McNairs of Virginia.

The people covered in that last section on Virginia are the focus of my book. But not all of them, because I did not want to include very distant cousins, their children, their children's children, and so on. I have narrowed the scope of inquiry to simply cover those individuals, and their siblings who are in a very direct line of descent from our earliest proven progenitor, Daniel McNair of Virginia. In following this format, what will emerge will not be so much a family tree with many branches waving in the breeze, but more of a totem pole, stacking family upon family, generation upon generation, from the first to today; standing on shoulders, and providing shoulders to stand upon, building the generations of "Us".

There have always been makers and shakers throughout history of course; people who change the world as it was previously known, in remarkable ways, people who create new societies out of whole cloth, new empires, new paradigms, or invent things that change lives forever, from Gutenberg's printing press to Oppenheimer's bomb, but they who do these things are few. For the rest of mankind, everyday lives did persist, and the lives they led can be likened to a bolt of cloth rolled out on a flat surface where each end of the bolt is indistinguishable from the other, where the lessons a person received in childhood from family and peers are the same lessons passed on to the generation that follows. Till the soil, plant the crops, provide care through the season and reap the harvest. Let some of the ground lie fallow, rotate the plantings---and repeat---and repeat---and repeat.

Until the early part of the twentieth century this was the life of most of the world's peoples, and even those who chose to live their life in the cities depended heavily upon the agrarian pursuits of their country kinfolk. But now is different. The majority of people in developed nations now live in urban locales, and a small minority of mega-farmers provides massive amounts of food to them, thanks to extreme technological modernization. Now, technology develops so fast that people are free to choose productive lives from a vast array of vocations and avocations. In today's world we are no longer tethered to the soil, unless we so choose, and that can be a wonderful choice, but we can also choose to live extraordinary lives, live in exotic climes, change the world and create remarkable inventions, art, and literature. I find the McNair legacy alive and well, thriving, and vibrant, and have high hopes for the future generations of "Us".

There will be no index for this book. If you are a living member of this history when published in 2015, you will find your name in chapters five or six (With apologies to the cousins I may have missed). You can start there and work backwards in time if you wish, but I would recommend starting in chapter one and learning your history as it happened chronologically. For privacy, living persons will be shown only with a year of birth rather than a full birth date, with the exception of my brothers and me, because we really don't give a rat's _ _ _.

I have dedicated this book to my brothers and to our brood, but of course there are now grandchildren and even great-grandchildren, and more will follow. Hallelujah! Perhaps some of them will one day add to my squiggles to keep the history current and vital, for they shall be forefathers and foremothers too.

Prologue

This prologue is being added at a point when this book is quite nearly completed, as this is information I have acquired only at this late stage. For over two decades I have been searching for the ancestry of Daniel McNair, our first proven progenitor, who settled in the Shenandoah Valley in Virginia in 1738. The information here given is unproven by me and so I am obliged to say that it can only be considered as speculation until it can be verified. I would like to say it is what I have sought, but cannot; however, I will say it holds more promise than other leads I have followed. With that caveat, this is what I have found. **John McNair,** born in 1664-1665 in Scotland, was a Covenanter, that is, a follower of the Presbyterian faith, who suffered the religious persecution of those who would try to force the Presbyterians to conform to the doctrines of the Church of England. The Covenanters refused, and held their secret worship services in the forests of the Scottish Highlands rather than submit to their oppressors. In Scotland the McNAIRS belonged to a gathering of clans of which the Earls of Lennox were the hereditary chieftains. Their gathering place was at the head of Loch Lomond. Eventually the persecution became so dire that John McNair moved, about 1688, from his ancestral home on the banks of the River Dee near it's conjunction with Loch Lomond, to the Parish Taboyne in County Donegal, Ireland. Here he obtained a farm called "Blanket Nuc" with a three-lives lease, which allowed for possession throughout John's life, then his son's life, and then his grandson's. This was a common arrangement at that time.

John's wife, whose name is as yet undiscovered, blessed him with four sons - John, Samuel, Robert, and **David**, between 1690 and 1695, all in Ireland. The death of John, about 1730, brought to an end the first life of the three-life lease, and at that time the Taboyne schoolmaster was brought in to regulate the family accounts. The chest containing the lease was produced and, unbeknownst to the family, the lease was stolen by the schoolmaster who then went to London where he forged a new lease and sold it to a Squire Howard, who then dispatched his agent to Ireland to cause surrender of the property or to secure a new lease at higher terms. (This chest, filled with very old family papers, is supposedly preserved at "Elmwood", Sonyea, N.Y., where some of the McNairs emigrated from Pennsylvania. The document alleging this is over 100 years old, and I can find no modern reference to this place.)

When John, the eldest son, found that he could not produce the original lease, he chose to take his family, leave Ireland, and resettle in the American colony of Pennsylvania in 1732. He was soon followed by his brothers and their families. John's son David, whose wife's name is also unknown, had at least six sons; **Daniel** born in Ireland in 1715, and also Alexander, William, Ezekiel, John, (born in Pennsylvania in 1734 and married Anne Davidson), and David Jr., born Dec 18th, 1736, who married Anna Maria Dunning.

This is where the speculation becomes the greatest. Our progenitor, **Daniel**, whom we will meet in chapter one, would definitely be a good match for the 1715 birthdate, and, in chapter one, we will also see that Daniel had on the gatepost of his plantation a sundial marked David McNare 2nd, and dated 1711. If we can one day determine that David had a first-born son named David, who was born, or perhaps died, in 1711, who did not survive to adulthood and was commemorated by the sundial, (meaning the sundial was for Daniels brother rather than his father) then this family line could well add two additional generations to our family totem, being **John the Covenanter**, and his son **David**. We can readily discount the fact that David had a son named David Jr. as his last known child, for it was not uncommon for a family to repeat the same name for a later child that had first been given to an earlier child who had not survived. Now, on to chapter one written before this prologue.

Chapter 1
Daniel and Hannah

Daniel McNair was among the very earliest pioneers in the Shenandoah Valley in Virginia, living in what was to become Augusta County at a later date. The land he settled on was part of the property which had been granted by the King of England to Benjamin Borden in an initial size of nearly 100,000 acres, which grew over time to 600,000 acres in the area of present day Rockbridge and Augusta counties. This was part of the Shenandoah Valley, bordered on the east by the Blue Ridge Mountains and on the west by the Allegheny Highlands (Appalachian Mountains).

The records in the suit of James Bell v. Bordens Executor's (Court Papers, 389, Augusta County, Virginia) give a clear account of the manner in which the tract of land was settled. On February 21, 1738, Alexander Brackenridge and George James, Robert and Adam Brackenridge, John Moore, Quantin Moore, George Henderson, James Bell (the Plaintiff), John Mackellan (Bell's servant), James Wattes, William McCanless, Robert Poage, Seth Poage, **Daniel McNair,** and John Graves, made a contract with Benjamin Borden, Sr., in which they agreed to build a small log house and make improvements upon the land, in return for which they were each to receive 200 acres of land.

This was evidently one of the first steps taken by Benjamin Borden, Sr., to colonize the grant. The parties named came to Augusta County in the year 1738. Some of them changed locations prior to 1745. Alexander Brackenridge made his permanent home on Lewis Creek, about two miles below Staunton. Robert Poage settled on the "Pennsylvania road" or "Irish Path" as the present Valley Turnpike was then called, about three miles north of Staunton. James Bell settled at the head of Long Glade, about ten miles north of Staunton; and **Daniel McNair** settled on Jenning's Branch in the neighborhood of present Churchville, Augusta County, settling in what would become known as the Stone Church neighborhood.
Robert Poage and James Bell were among the first members of the county court of Augusta County, and Daniel McNair was a Captain of Militia by 1747. Daniel married a woman whose given name was Hannah. Ephraim McDowell, the original surveyor of the grant, and his family

15

along with John Lewis and his family, are the only settlers who are definitely known to have preceded these parties as settlers upon the Borden grant, arriving there perhaps as early as 1732.

Various purchases and sales of land, both to and from Daniel and Hannah, are recorded in court records from these early years, which increased the McNair holdings to approximately 700 acres on the waterways known then as Middle River, Borden Creek, and Jenning's Branch. Following here are a few of those entries:

> To Daniel McEnere--30 March, 1743-- 400 Acres on a branch of the James River called Borden's Creek (Book 21, Page 251, Augusta Co, Patents).
> To Daniel McNare--20 September, 1748 -- 27 Acres on the Middle River of Shanando & 29 Acres on the Middle River of Shanando (Book 28, Pages 381 & 382)

> 31st December, 1745. Daniel McEnaire (McNare). Gent to James Trimble, surveyor, £22, 10 shillings Virginia money; 400 acres on a branch of James River called Burden's Creek. Witnesses, James Sayers, David Trimble, Silas Hart. Acknowledged by Daniel McNare and Hannah, his wife 11th February, 1745-6.

> 27th August, 1751. Daniel McNare to David Sayers, 23 acres Mid. Riv. Shanandore; patented to Daniel, 20th September, 1748.

> 23d November, 1753. James Patton to Daniel McAnare, 390 acres on a branch of Woods River; corner. Wm. Sayers.

> 29th May, 1750. Daniel McAnaire and Hannah to James Sayers. £80, 147 acres, part of 400 patented to Daniel, 10th June, 1740 and bounded by a tract laid off for Thos. Gardner on west and one for Alex Gibson on east. Teste: Jean Beard, William Christell. Delivered: Sampson Archer, November, 1759.

> 21st October, 1765. Daniel McAnare and Hannah to Buchanan and Thompson, executors of Col. James Patton, £100, 390 acres on a branch of Woods River, part of a large tract patented to Col. James Patton; corner land of Wm. Sayers; corner Harman's land. Delivered: William Campbell, December, 1770.

> 21st October, 1765. James Sayers and Rachel to Daniel McAnare, £200, 140 acres, part of 400 patented to Daniel, 10th June, 1740, and conveyed to James, 29th May, 1756, bounded by tract laid off for Thomas Gardner, also a tract laid off for Alex. Gibson. Delivered: Daniel McAnare, 4th January, 1773.

On Jennings Branch and Middle River, 625 acres patented to Daniel McNare 1st February, 1781; also 96 acres patented to said Daniel 20th July, 1768. Teste: Rebekah and Hanna Sawyers, Wm. Buchanan.

Multiple spellings of Daniel's surname are noted in these early records, including those just shown, plus McAnore, McAnair, McNair, and McEnaire. Names were recorded by clerks and clerics alike, as they heard them, and seeing these different spellings almost lets us *hear* the brogue that rolled off the tongues of Daniel and his Scot-Irish neighbors. It is unfortunate, however, that we do not know whether Daniel's brogue was fully Scottish or tinged from time in Ireland. The McNair clan definitely originated in Scotland, but religious persecution had driven many, though not all, of those Scot born McNairs to Ireland many years before they crossed the water to the New World of the American colonies. For instance, in a book titled *Families of County Donegal, Ireland* by Michael C. O'Laughlin is this entry: "The civil survey of 1654 finds a house and garden in Raphoe, held by the executors of Patricke McNare, a British Protestant."

The property that Daniel accumulated beginning in 1738 stayed in the hands of his descendants for many years. Daniel passed his land and home to his eldest son David. David's inheritance passed on to his son James, who in turn provided the family plantation, consisting of the home and over 700 acres, to his sons James Newton McNair and Richard Henry McNair. According to the 1900 U.S. census, James Newton McNair was born in February, 1838, so he would have been eighty-three years of age when he sold the last of the property to a man named Roy Simmons on October 27, 1921. Thus ended 183 years of continuous ownership of the original Virginia plantation of the McNairs. James Newton McNair died six years later on December 29, 1927.

The name David, as son of Daniel, in the above citation, is one indication of the *possible* name of Daniel's father, namely David McNair. A particular naming pattern for the Scot-Irish of that time was to name the firstborn son for the father's father. Another indication is a small sundial that was mounted for many years on the gatepost of the McNair plantation. That sundial is engraved "David McNare, 2nd, 1711". As noted in that McNair genealogy written by James Birtley McNair, that sundial is in the possession of the Stover family in Virginia, descendants of

Daniel McNair and family lore says that the sundial did belong to Daniel's father. If that is true, then the sundial also tells us the name of Daniel's grandfather, namely David McNair, 1st [Sr.].

Speculating on those names however, is simply that---speculation. (see the prologue for another possible explanation) The 1711 date is of course of no help, because we cannot know what the date commemorates. It is certainly too late a date to be the birth date of Daniel's father, for with Daniel of an age to be pioneering land in 1738, his own birth would likely have been between 1700 and 1720. The date may indicate David's arrival in the colonies (most likely Pennsylvania) or simply be the year the sundial was created. The sundial may have been intended for a brother of Daniel's, for some other kinfolk, or even for Daniel himself, being a given name that he chose not to use. That the name of Daniel's father and grandfather was David is *very* likely, but is as yet unproven. Please see the prologue to this book which gives a postulation of who these early Davids were and their connection back into Scotland.

Whatever the names, though, there can be no doubt as to the strength, tenacity, and character of the hearty souls who entered upon the task of carving a home out of the wilderness that they committed their lives to achieve. Fertile soil and ample water awaited them in the Shenandoah Valley, but so did almost unimaginable threats and dangers. Wildlife was abundant to put meat in the stewpot, but some of the game there was as likely to eat them, as to be eaten by them. And, of course, the settlers were the first Europeans to take up residence, but they were far from being the first people in the valley. By the early part of the eighteenth century, when the Europeans began to arrive in numbers, internal fighting among the native tribes had caused the Indian people to abandon the valley as a place to live, and to use it instead as their hunting ground. Shawnee, Iroquois, Monacans, Occoneechee, and Piscataway all hunted in the area; It is easy to understand how the white man's presence there, clearing land to farm, building shelters, roads and bridges, and harvesting game from the forests, was considered a direct assault on the native's livelihood.

On many occasions the settlements were attacked, men killed, women and children abducted, crops destroyed, and homes burned to the ground. Today it may seem easy to abhor the actions taken by the natives, but should also be easy to understand the motive driving them to these actions, as their very way of life was threatened by the advance of the white settlers. By fortune and fortitude the McNair family apparently was spared during these attacks, as I find no record of them suffering such losses.

Due to the nature of the dangers faced, the men did form militias to protect themselves and their families. Daniel McNair served as a Private, an Ensign, and by 1747 was a Captain of militia. Farming the fertile soil was the occupation followed by almost all of the inhabitants, but the community could not thrive on agriculture alone. Many of the settlers contributed their talents, and supplemented their incomes, through additional labors. Materials and goods that could not be provided from within had to be obtained from Pennsylvania or the settlements of eastern Virginia, either being an arduous and dangerous trek, and so blacksmiths, farriers, gunsmiths, surveyors, hunters, trappers, and others rose from within their ranks to fill the communities' needs. Daniel McNair was a miller, grinding the grain grown by his neighbors as well as his own. These were men who wished to bestow upon themselves and their families the fruits of their own labors, and in the earliest years they were able, for the most part, to do just that. In time, however, the population grew to a size that made them a viable and valuable market for merchants outside their valley. Just fifteen years after his arrival, Daniel was adding his name to a petition to the 1753-54 session of the Augusta Court, in an attempt to hold at bay outside influences that were threatening the livelihood of those growing grain in the valley:

1753-4 Session
To the Worshipful Court of Augusta now sitting: We, the inhabitants of this County, have long felt the smart of the great indulgence the ordinary keepers of this County have met with in allowing them to sell such large quantities of rum and wine at an extravagant rate, by which our money is drained out of the County, for which we have no return but a fresh supply to pick our pockets. We, your petitioners, humbly pray your worship to put a stop to the said liquors, which would encourage us to pursue our laborious designs, which is to raise sufficient quantities of grain which would sufficiently supply us with liquors and the money circulate in this County to the advantage of us, the same. We hope that your worships will discover to us that you have a real regard for the good of the County, and lay us under an obligation to pray for your prosperity.
Signed---
Robert Stevenson, James Hamilton, Alexander Walker, James Robertson, James Stevenson, John Christian. Alexander Blair, Thomas Shiels, Robert Christian, Thomas Stewart, James Allen, Joseph Hanna, Francis Beaty, Mathew Lyle,

Archibald Reah, John Walker, Samuel Downey, John Anderson, **Daniel McAnair (McNair)**, Robert Spears (Sayers), Daniel Danison, and 63 other signers.

Of course, whether rum and wine from abroad, or whiskey and bourbon from his own corn and grain, we also learn from the records that Daniel was not opposed to an occasional nip, and that he had just a wee bit of a feisty streak.

> JANUARY 28, 1766   Daniel McAnare misbehaved by appearing in Court drunk and giving Gabriel Jones, gent., Deputy Attorney for the King, the lie, and likewise insulting the Court.

I have found no evidence that Daniel ever owned any slaves, nor had any indentured servants, although he may have, as both practices were common in Virginia, yet less so in the Valley than in the eastern part of the Colony. The following citation then, binding a young girl to Daniel, may have been an indenture, or may have been more akin to an adoption, or caretaker position:

> AUGUST 17, 1769.
> Catharine Sawyers, orphan of Alexander Sawyers, aged 15 last March,
> to be bound to Daniel McNare.

Initially the religious needs of the area were met by circuit riding ministers, who would come to them from Pennsylvania, providing them with services wherever they could meet, be it in their homes or even in open meadows or pastures. Over time the settlements grew and the men and women within them felt the need to establish permanent houses of worship, with the hope of recruiting a minister who would stay in their midst. They formed the Congregation of the Triple Forks of the Shenandoah in 1740, and built two meeting houses, called the Augusta Stone Church (1740) and Tinkling Spring (1745). The original structure at Augusta Stone was a log building, as it was at Tinkling Spring, but between 1747 and 1749, the Augusta Church was rebuilt in stone, and it is still in service now nearly 270 years later, standing as the oldest continually operating Presbyterian Church in Virginia. Daniel McNair was involved in the construction of both of these churches. The minister who conducted the services at both of the churches was Reverend John Craig.

Much of Rev. Craig's baptismal registers have been preserved, and on occasion the he left us with some interesting insights about the growing community he served. At the end of 1740, John Craig writes, "The year being ended, the whole number baptized by me is one hundred and thirty-three: sixty-nine males and sixty-four females. Glory to God who is daily adding members to His visible church!"   It should be noted here that not all of the occupants of the valley were freemen or there by their own choice. There was a practice among the magistrates of the British Isles to impose a sentence of "Transportation" on criminals convicted in their jurisdictions, causing them to serve out their sentences as indentured servants in the American colonies, thus removing them from Great Britain, and at the same time providing the colonists with a much needed source of inexpensive laborers. This was a good arrangement for all concerned, assuming, of course, that you were not the criminal.   Nonetheless, this did introduce men and women of low moral character into the colonies including the Shenandoah Valley. But good people appear to have sought to rear the children of the convicts under religious influences. On January 20, 1742, Rev. Craig writes: "Mr. James Patton stood sponsor for a child baptized, named Henry, born in his house of a convict servant, a base person; could not be brought to tell who was the father, notwithstanding all means used."

Further, we learn from the register that Robert, son of Robert Young, was baptized January 22, 1742, and Mr. Craig notes that he was "born with teeth."

In the second year the number of baptisms was eighty-two, and the record is followed by another inscription of praise to God.

On December 19, 1742, we find: "This day the news of the Indian rebellion and the death of our friends by their hands came to our ears", making note of the massacre of John McDowell and his companions in the Forks of the James River.

The number of inhabitants continued to grow, and during the year 1749, besides his regular preaching places, Augusta Stone and Tinkling Spring, Rev. Craig administered baptism at North Mountain, South Mountain, Timber Grove, North River, near Great Lick, and at Calf Pasture and Cow Pasture.

The last entry in the book is dated September 28, 1749. During the nine preceding years the number of baptisms was 883; 463 males and 420 females.

Baptisms are recorded for three of the four children born to Daniel and Hannah McNair. There is no record for the eldest son David, who was probably born in 1740, perhaps before the baptismal record began. The next two children were daughters: Joanna was baptized on the 19th of December, 1742, and Martha was baptized on the 30th of June, 1745. James McNair was baptized on the 29th of April, 1747. There may have been other children born to the couple, but no record has come down to us. Thus the family tree begins:

- David McNair, was born about 1740
- Joanna McNair, bapt. 19 December 1742   *[the day of the Indian rebellion]*
- Martha McNair, bapt. 30 June 1745
- **James McNair**, bapt.   29 April 1747

The Augusta Stone Church built in 1747-1749,
replacing the original log structure. Still in use as of 2015

James McNair is next in the paternal lineage that we will be tracing in chapter two, but we will spend some time first considering his older brother David, who was apparently Daniel's first-born. As previously noted, it was David who inherited his father's land and home, and this was in keeping with the commonly practiced inheritance "Law of Primogeniture," in which virtually all of a man's property passed to his eldest living son upon his death, with minimal amounts bequeathed

22

to the remaining children. Oftentimes, the widow stayed on in the home and was cared for by the inheriting son until her death or remarriage.

David McNair, like his father, was a literate man, able to read and write and cipher well, and his name appears frequently in the court records of Augusta County as testator or witness or appraiser of property transactions, wills, and appraisals of properties both Real and personal as devised in those wills. Ironically, David died in 1805 without having written a will for himself. However, he was the executor of his father's will, and performed the appraisal as well.

JULY 19, 1791.
Admn. of estate of Daniel McNair granted David McNair.

(Note--with Daniel's death apparently occurring in 1791, we can guess that he lived into his seventies or possibly even his eighties.)

The appraisement of Daniel McNair's estate was recorded on the 20th of September, 1791, and included a Note (loan) on John Knowles, and business accounts vs. George Lebum, Owen Colley, Michael Dwier, Niclas Suesanger, and Tolly Divat, for services, probably being the milling of their grain.

David McNair, five years before this, had been married to a woman who might have been his cousin, since his mother Hannah's maiden name *may* have been Allen. His marriage was to Elizabeth Allen, the daughter of Capt. James Allen Sr. (The Virginia Magazine of History claims *Daniel's* wife was Hannah Allen, daughter of Capt. James Allen Sr., but I can find no independent confirmation of that at all, and I believe them to possibly be in error, having inadvertently mixed the records of father and son.) However, the proof of marriage for David is not in question. In the court records, we find the marriage banns, and the marriage itself:

November 8, 1786
David McNair and Betty Allen, daughter of James Allen; surety,
Francis Allen; witnesses, Fras. Allen, Poley Allen, Rebeckah Allen.

December 19, 1786
David McNare and Elizabeth Allen; married.

Less than two years after marrying James' daughter, David was one of the executors of his father-in-law's will.

28th April, 1788. James Allen's will (Sr.),farmer--To children of daughter, Rachel Thomson, 5 shillings each; to daughter, Margaret Bell, 5 shillings; to daughter, Agnes Shields, 6 shillings, to son, William Bell, 5 shillings; to daughter, Rebecca McClure, 5 shillings; to daughter, **Elizabeth McNair**, 5 shillings; to daughter, Mary Allen, 5 shillings; to son, Francis Allen, £50; to son, James, home plantation. Executors, wife Mary, son-in-law David McNaire, son James.
Teste: Wm. Wilson, James Allen, John Hartsook, Wm. Baker. Codicil,
24th March, 1789. Teste: Wm. Wilson, John Hartsook, Wm. Baker. Proved, 18th October, 1791, by Hartsook and Baker.

Here again, we see that the eldest son, in this case James Allen Jr., was the sole beneficiary of the home plantation.

David McNair served as a Lieutenant in Trimble's company during the Revolutionary War. Then, during the war of 1812, he served his country again as Captain of the 7th Company in Barbee's Regiment of the Kentucky Militia. His Lieutenant in those latter campaigns was George Allen, and his Ensign was Nimrod Maxwell, all from the Fort Defiance, Augusta County area.

This area is referred to as Fort Defiance, but that is somewhat of a misnomer. The Augusta Stone Church was, on more than one occasion, used as a safe refuge when there was threat of possible Indian attack, but there is no record that any actual attack was ever directed at that building, and no fort by that name was ever constructed. Years after these heady days had passed, there was laid the Valley Railroad, and on that line, about 500 to 600 yards away from the Stone Church, the rail station was given the name "Fort Defiance".

David and Elizabeth were the parents of ten children:

- Daniel McNair, who died before 1805.
- James McNair was born about 1788-89, and married Lydia Roundabush. This couple had six children:
- Margaret (Polly) McNair
- Elizabeth (Betsy) McNair
- Ward McNair married Catherine Haines in 1826 and they had ten children.

24

- Hannah McNair married John Burgess. They had a son and two daughters.
- Martha McNair
- David McNair, who died unmarried in 1822, and left all of his property to his elder brother James.
- William McNair
- John McNair married Anne Hogshead in 1825. They had six children.

Finally, before we leave Augusta County to follow Daniel's son **James** into Kentucky and Tennessee, here is an interesting item about the Middle River area where the McNair plantation arose. From the book *ANNALS OF AUGUSTA COUNTY, Supplement of 1888 by Jos. A. Waddell:*

> The most interesting part of Augusta County, in some respects, is the strip of country extending from the iron bridge across Middle river, on the Staunton and Churchville road, up the river to the mouth of Buffalo Branch, and up that stream and Dry Branch to their respective sources. Middle river is throughout its whole extent in Augusta. From its head spring, near Shemariah church, to its mouth, near Mount Meridian, is only about thirty-five miles; but the length of the stream, in its meanderings, is not far short of a hundred miles.
> Beginning as a mountain rill, it broadens as it goes, and towards its mouth becomes a wide and beautiful river. On the west side of the river, a little beyond the bridge, on the Dudley farm, is what remains of an ancient artificial mound. It has been plowed over for many years, and is now nearly leveled. Human bones, pipes, and stone arrow-heads have often been turned up. It is supposed that, before the arrival of white people in the Valley, a battle between Indians occurred at the spot, and that the slain were buried there.

As noted above, this was written in 1888, but it was not until 1894 that the first mounds attributed to Native American "mound-builders" were excavated by Cyrus Thompson of the Smithsonian Institution. These mounds are attributed to numerous and various tribes, spread from the Great Lakes to the Gulf of Mexico, and from the Mississippi River to the Appalachians, spanning a timeframe from 300 BCE to 1200 A.D. Their purpose and meaning are thought to be religious and/or ceremonial, and they were frequently used as burial sites.

Chapter 2   James and Martha

James McNair, if born in 1747, (the year of his baptism), would have been just twenty-one years old when he first struck out on his own.   In the fall of 1768, James, along with John Anderson, William Anderson, John Sawyer, Robert Christian, Gilbert Christian, and Nathan Page, explored the area of the Long Island of the Holston River in an area whose borders were disputed between the Virginia and North Carolina colonies. This area later became part of what is now Sullivan County, Tennessee. At a location on Reedy Creek, about one mile above where it fed into the Holston, they constructed cabins and wintered over in 1768-69. In the spring they planted corn and began additional improvements and structures. To their great disappointment by late summer they learned that they had located on land that was part of a large land grant previously awarded to Edmund Pendleton, a prior surveyor for the loyalist (British) government. Thus, they were forced to abandon their claims, and so returned for a time to Virginia. Had they been able to stay, they would have been the first white men to settle permanently in Tennessee.

On April 7th of 1773, James McNair took as his bride Martha Price, a young woman of Welsh extraction, born November 25, 1753, in Mecklenburg County, North Carolina to John and Mary (White) Price. Martha's paternal grandfather was Rice Price, who had been born in Cardiff, Wales, about 1690. In Scottish or Irish names, "Mac" or "Mc" was used to denote "the child of", but in Welsh naming patterns, the choice was "ap." Thus, a son named Rice (in the Welsh tongue, Rhys) whose father's name was also Rice, would have been called Rice ap Rice. As the Welsh names and language assimilated into Colonial America, the "ap Rice" simply became "Price."

James and Martha now moved back near the Holston River settlements along with John Anderson, who was James McNair's childhood friend on Middle River, and who had been with him on the earlier sojourn into the Holston wilderness. John Anderson married Rebecca Maxwell on the 12th of June, 1775. Years later, James' daughter Elizabeth (Betsy) would marry John's son, John Anderson Jr.   In 1775, John Anderson moved to the North Fork of the Holston, and constructed there a fortified blockhouse which became the starting point of the famed Wilderness Trail. Starting that same year, Daniel Boone and a crew of thirty ax-men carved that trail from the Anderson Blockhouse through Moccasin Gap, through what would become Kentucky, and through

27

the Cumberland Gap back into Tennessee. There were a number of additional fortifications being built at this time, because the opening of this frontier was now in full swing, and the Scot-Irish, German, and English settlers were pouring into Western Virginia and North Carolina; into the fertile lands that would eventually become Kentucky and Tennessee.

James McNair was a Free Mason, and he served in the militia on the frontier of the North Carolina colony as an Indian fighter, and continued in his service during the Revolutionary War. For his service he received grants of land, and he acquired additional land by purchase throughout the 1780's, acquiring holdings in present day Sullivan, Hawkins, and Greene counties, Tennessee, and in Kentucky on the Wilderness Road. The Kentucky lands, totaling 1400 acres were secured in partnership with another settler from Augusta County, James Trimble. In the early 1790's he moved into Knox County, Tennessee, and acquired land there. James was active in the civic life of Knoxville and Knox County. The minutes of the county, 1792-95, show that he served as a Juryman August 6, 1794. Legal documents show that he was active in public affairs in the County until his death. His will was written in his own hand January 5, 1817, and proved at the July term of the County court, 1818. The will in full is recorded in the Knox Co. Estate Book, Vol. 2, pages 351 and 352. His wife's will was written March 23, 1817, and was proved at the same session of the Court. The following is the transcription of his will:

> In the name of God, Amen. I, James McNair of the County of Knox, State of Tennessee, being in a low state of health, but of sound memory, do make this my Last Will and Testament. I First of all resign my soul to God the giver in hopes for mercy at the great day , and for my worldly affairs I dispose of them as followith: I wish all my just debts and funeral charges to be paid from my moveable property and my daughter Myre to have a horse worth 100 dollars or the money. To my true and well beloved wife, Martha, I give and bequeath my dwelling house as it stands with all and every part of furniture, the kitchen, smoke house, crib and Garden and the half of all kind of stock and farm tools, also old Cipeo, Rhoda and her child Cubit, all of which is to be at her disposal in her life time or at her death. I do will that my land at the death of my wife be sold to the highest bidder and also my boys, Bob and Austin, and from the sale, my son John is to have and receive one half of the purchase money, my son James Fleris one third, my son David and my daughters Polly, Hannah, Betsy and Myre shall have equal shares of the other third part. My son John is to have one half of the stock and all utensils with his mother and have full care of her. He has Bob and Austin as assistants and the whole

plantation to cultivate for which he, the said John, is to let her have a full third part of all produce. I choose my true and trusted friends Asahel Chapman and my son John as my executors to see that my last will and testament be carefully executed. All former wills being made void and of no effect. This I say, is my last will and testament wrote with my own hand and sealed with my seal this 5th day of January in the year of our Lord one thousand eight hundred and seventeen. Signed Jas. M'Nair, in the presence of Ro. Armstrong, Fras. Bounds.

James would have been almost 70 years of age at the time of his death, and Martha would have been 63 at hers, she having been born November 25th, 1753.

We must note here the first documented instance of slaveholding by a McNair. There are five slaves, all mentioned by name in the above will. Old Cipeo, Rhoda, and her child Cubit, were willed to Martha directly, whereas Bob and Austin were to assist son John in the operation of the plantation, for the benefit of both John and his mother. In Martha's will, there is mention of a slave boy named Greene, but in the inventory of James' property it is clear that Greene and Cubit are one and the same, that is, the son of Rhoda. We can gain thought-provoking insight into the lives of our forefathers when we look at the inventory that was presented to the court for the settlement of James McNair's last will and testament by the executors Ashel Chapman and his son, John McNair. The inventory paints a picture of labor and frugality, of toil and struggle, but in the company of success gained in the face of adversity. In his day, James would have been considered a relatively wealthy and influential man. So now close your eyes, let your imagination wander, turn off your gas and electric, cable and internet, sell your car, and move yourself and family onto this acreage with only these worldly goods ---- for the rest of your life! Would you survive it?

First, 520 acres of land, one negro man named Sippio, one negro woman named Rhoda and her child named Greene, two negro boys named Bob and Austin, four head of horses, thirteen head of cows, and fifteen head of sheep, thirty head of hogs, six hogsheads, [large barrels or casks] one waggon and two pair of geers, [for hitching horses, mules or oxen to the wagon] four ploughs, four hoes, one log chain, one pair of stretchers, one iron wedge, two axes, one frow, [a tool with a wedge shaped blade] one crowbar, one crosscut saw, one hand-saw, two augers, two chisels, one stake, two hammers, three cubbirds [cupboards] and furniture, two trunks, one box, seven chairs, two pair of steel aids, one salt pan and kittle, two pots, three ovens, two skillits, two pot-racks, one pair of fire tongs and shovel, one pair waffle-irons, one grid iron, three tables, one desk, four spinning wheels, one loom and harness, one saddle, one looking-glass, one gallon measure, one lantern, three pails, two coolers, one churn, two barrels, one flax-break, one set of harrow teeth, two smoothing irons, two pair of fire-dogs, [andirons] one coffee mill, one teakettle, one cutting box and knife, two drawing knives, four beds, bedsteads and furniture.

Two pieces of family lore have come down over the years about James and Martha, and while I cannot vouch for their accuracy, they are entertaining and so I include them here for your pleasure. The very nature of the lives that pioneer families led oftentimes caused the man of the household to be away from home for extended periods of time. On one such occasion, Martha heard the dogs barking, and when she went to discover the cause, she found that the dogs had treed a bear. Returning to the house to retrieve her gun, Martha soon put an end to the bear, and without assistance skinned Mr. Bruin and prepared the meat for the smokehouse and cook pit.

In another instance, James returned from an absence to learn that his horses had been stolen by Indians. Early the following morning he began a pursuit and, after tracking them for three days, he came upon their camp and killed two of them while the rest made their escape. James recaptured his horses and safely returned to his home.

Seven children of James and Martha are mentioned in James' will, and there was at least one other son, named Price, who died the year before his father's will was written. Price died intestate (no written will) but his brother John did do an inventory of his estate and it was recorded on page 272 of will book 2, at the October, 1816 term of the Knox County court. The brief inventory showed only the following: "One Land Warrant of 122 &1/2 acres, one saddle, and one Gun Barrel." Tennessee military records show that Price was a Private in Johnson's 3rd regiment, East Tennessee Militia, during the war of 1812.

There may have been other children born to James McNair and Martha Price, but I find no record of any but these eight. Thus the family tree continues:

In the future Sullivan County, Tennessee:

- David McNair was born in 1774;
- Mary (Polly) McNair was born January 10, 1776;
- James Fleris McNair was born in 1780;

30

- Hannah McNair was born in 1781 or 1782;
- John (Jack) McNair was born July29, 1783;
- Elizabeth (Betsy) was born March 31. 1785;

And in the future Knox County, Tennessee:

- Myra McNair was born in 1790;
- Price McNair was born in 1792.

John McNair is next in our direct paternal lineage, but first we will consider his siblings, briefly for all but David, whose story is of more than passing interest.

David McNair was married on December 30, 1801 in Knox County to a woman named Delilah Amelia Vann, who was the daughter of a Cherokee Indian Chief named James Clement Vann. He was the son of a white trader named John Joseph Vann, and a Cherokee woman named Wah-Li.

After their marriage, David and Delilah moved to the Ocoee District, part of the Cherokee Nation in Southeast Tennessee, which in 1836 would become Bradley County, during the forced removal (Trail of Tears) of the Indians to the "New Indian Country" which would become, eventually, the state of Oklahoma.

David was an industrious, ambitious, and capable man and established a farm on the banks of the Consauga River. By 1820 he had opened a store and tavern, and a boatyard on this property, and created an overland portage between his boatyard on the south, and the boatyard of Michael Hildebrand on the Ocoee River, twelve miles to the north. These two men built enormous wagons capable of moving flat-bottomed keelboats fully fifty feet in length, six feet in width and six feet in depth, without the need to unload the cargo onboard. The wagon so loaded required up to six span of oxen to move that weight. This greatly shortened the travel distance and time for traders who were moving their goods from the Ohio River, by way of the Kentucky and Tennessee Rivers, to the Ocoee River. After crossing this twelve mile portage, the traders could leave McNair's boatyard and travel down the Consauga River to the trading centers on the Gulf of Mexico.

In the Cherokee Nation, talent and leadership were more important than pure bloodlines, and David showed these qualities well. During the War of 1812 he served as a spy, and as a Captain of two troops of Cherokee, in battles against the Creek Indians, who had allied themselves with the

British during that conflict. David's accomplishments not only made him a wealthy man, but even allowed him to rise to become a Cherokee Chief himself, like his father-in-law, James Vann. (Being a chief was much like being a mayor.)

David and Delilah's property was located just over a mile north of the Georgia border where they had built a two-storey brick home, along with a brick smokehouse, and even brick quarters for his slaves. I can find no record of the actual number of slaves held by David, because the Federal Census for 1820 and 1830 did not cover the Cherokee Nation, but I have seen speculation that the number may have been upward of fifty.

The home survived for nearly one hundred years after the deaths of David and Delilah until it was severely damaged by a tornado in 1932, and torn down in 1933.

Home of David McNair near Tennga, Tenn.

David and his wife were the parents of six children, whose names were Elizabeth, James Vann, Nicholas Byers, Martha P., Clement Vann, and Mary Vann McNair. These children and their families were part of the Cherokee Nation and were forced out of their homes onto the Trail of Tears, the great removal heartbreak.

I am going to include here the text of a letter written by John Coffee to the Governor of Georgia, Wilson Lumpkin, written in July of 1832:

Head Quarters, Etowah, Cherokee Nation   July 21st. 1832.
Governor Wilson Lumpkin, Milledgeville, .Georgia
Sir;
Your letter dated the 10th Instant, I have the honor to acknowledge, by yesterdays mail. I cannot but express my surprise that the letter written by Mr. Brown had not arrived, as he informed me that it was written immediately on his release.
Mr. Brown was arrested by virtue of an order from John Ross, [A principle Cherokee Chief] and directed to James McNair, Nicholas McNair, & Rily Thornton, directing them to arrest some one of the Georgia Surveyors, and carry him before Esqr. McConnell of Tennessee, to be tried for a violation of the intercourse law of 1802.   James McNair was confined by a rheumatic affliction; this was the cause of Old McNair's agency in the affair. Pursuant to their directions they carried Mr. Brown before Esqr. McConnell of Tennessee, who issued his warrant and had him placed under the care of an officer. Mr. Brown   chose to be carried before Judge Keith of the district court of the U. S. for East Tennessee. Judge Keith refused to have anything to do with him. Mr. Brown was then conducted before Esqr. Johnston, who committed him to the custody of the Jailer of Athens, Tennessee. In the mean time Mr. Brown was informed that Judge Keith would not object to hearing the case if he was brought before him by a habeas corpus, this was done, and after a full investigation of the matter Mr. Brown was discharged. The whole of the proceedings occupied from Wednesday   until the following Monday, all of which time Brown was in custody.
These are the facts of the arrest, & trial as I understand them, and I have no doubt but will be fully established before the court when necessary. My reasons for postponing the arrest of the persons engaged in this matter, you are already in possession of, and I hope will approve them. Old McNair passed through this neighborhood a few days since, and wrote me a note. I went to see him, and rode with him several miles; he was on his way to Rogers's. I have heard from them some and they are in favor of a treaty. He will go by Dave Vanns, & Ross's to the council, and I have no doubt but he feels as much interest in bringing about a treaty as yourself, And I have now but little doubt but it will be accomplished. All the principal Chiefs in this part of the nation are decidedly in favor of treating, and as far as I can learn this disposition is gaining rapidly all over the nation. Colonel Williamson has been several days visiting the chiefs in Oostanollee [Eastanollee, Georgia] and that neighborhood, and I have no doubt will do much good. I shall set

33

out in the morning and visit that part of the nation below the Alabama line, the Lookout Mountain. I have determined not to attend the council, but have made arrangements to obtain all the information from that meeting. I hope that your public duty will permit you to visit this post from Athens after the commencement, and stay until after the council adjourns, or should you propose to spend your time at some one of the neighboring villages, and will inform me which, Colonel Williamson, or myself will have the honor of waiting on you, & giving you all the information immediately after the council adjourns.

I have the honor to be most respectfully your Excellency's most Obdt. Servt.

[Signed] Jno. Coffee .

There are three McNairs mentioned in this letter. They are James Vann and Nicholas Byers, David McNair's two eldest sons, and "Old McNair", who is David himself. The treaty being discussed will eventually be called the Treaty of Echota, signed in 1835, which will create the forced removal of the Cherokee people and the ceding of their Tennessee and Georgia homeland to the United States. John Ross, whom David was going to see, was one of the prominent negotiators on the Cherokee side, and was very much against the proposed treaty. He was swayed, though, when, in addition to the new Cherokee Nation West land, a payment of twenty million dollars was promised. Only five million was ever paid. Further still, the Cherokee were to have a delegate in the U.S. House of Representatives. The treaty is still in effect today, but a Cherokee delegate has never been seated in the house. David McNair was a member of the council negotiating the treaty, and favored it, even though he knew that he and his family would be moved to the Oklahoma Territory as their new home. His brother **John** would end up living on David's farm in the former Cherokee Nation after David's death, and his children's removal. The completion of the treaty would have been more difficult, or even failed but for the fact that there was dissention within the tribe over the leadership of the tribe. President Andrew Jackson's delegates played upon the factionalism by holding multiple conferences with the various tribal factions, and in the end bypassed the leadership almost entirely to get a treaty signed. After Senate ratification, the removal began in earnest.

David had died when the removal was just beginning, and was buried on his own plantation, and later, Delilah, along with her daughters, had been taken away to await a boat that would begin their journey West. At the river crossing, Delilah died, and the Federal troops allowed the daughters to return her body to be buried alongside her husband. A number of years later, in 1846, some of the descendants of this proud couple returned from Oklahoma and placed a horizontal marble slab near their grave, and built a small limestone wall to completely surround it.

The marker reads as follows:

Sacred to the memory of David and Delilah A McNair, who departed this life, the former on the 15th of August, 1836, and the latter on the 30th of November, 1838. Their children, being members of the Cherokee Nation and having to go with their people to the West, do leave this monument, not only to show their regard for their parents, but to guard their sacred ashes against the unhallowed intrusion of the white man.

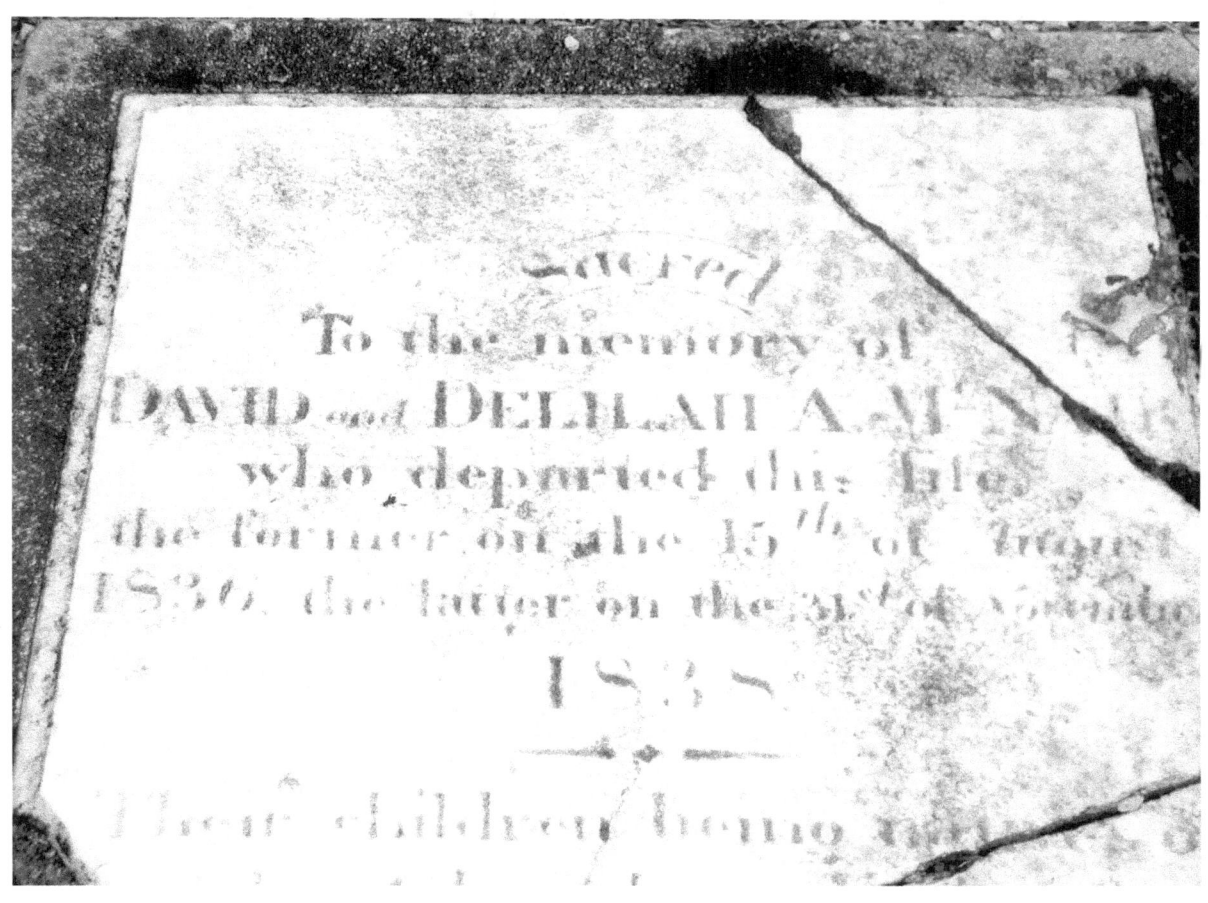

The marker

The limestone wall still stands strong after more than 160 years

Here for those who wish to find kinship with someone famous is information about Delilah Amelia Vann's niece, Sally Vann. Sally married a man named Robert Rogers. Robert and Sally were forced west to the Cherokee Nation West (now part of Oklahoma). There the couple had a child named Clement Vann Rogers, who in turn married a woman with the fanciful name of Mary America Schrimsher. This union produced eight children, the last of which, born in 1879, they named William Penn Adair Rogers, more commonly known as Will Rogers, the wonderful lasso-twirling cowboy humorist and folk philosopher of the early Twentieth Century.

James and Martha's second child was Mary (Polly) who married David Moore on June 10, 1794, in Knox County, where their first daughter Elizabeth Myra, was born in June of 1795. The couple then moved to Roane County, Tennessee, where they had three more daughters, followed by four sons. Their names were Melinda Ann, Hannah Margaret, Eliza Jane, David, Joseph, Thomas and William Samuel Moore. Mary passed away in 1852 at age 75.

Third was James Fleris McNair who married Rebecca Walker in Roane County on Jul 2, 1811; they had six children, Nancy, James Price, Narcissus, Susan, Tillie Mary, and David. James died in Chattanooga, TN on Aug 27, 1849.

Hannah McNair married Jesse C. Terry on March 31, 1797, and they had four children, named Mary, Sarah, Myra, and Jesse. Hannah died at age 78, in October of 1859, at Kingston, Roane County, Tennessee.

Elizabeth (Betsy) McNair married three times. Her first husband was John Anderson Jr., the son of John Anderson of the Blockhouse, the life-long friend of James and Martha. They were married in Knox County on November 12, 1805, and soon moved to Pikeville in Bledsoe County. They had six children there, named Louisa Maxwell, Josiah McNair, James Madison, Elizabeth Ann, Franklin, and John III Anderson. Elizabeth was pregnant with John III when her husband, who was a Lieutenant Colonel in the Tennessee militia, died as he was marching his regiment to New Orleans for the final battle of the War of 1812. Although the Treaty of Ghent (modern day Belgium) had been signed on Christmas Eve in 1814 to end the war, word did not reach the Gulf region in time to prevent the famous Battle of New Orleans in January of 1815.

Elizabeth next married James Thurman and had one daughter, Sophia. Her third marriage was to James Loyd, and they had Jane, Albert, Martha and Roland Loyd.

Myra McNair married William S. Howell on February 15, 1816. I have found no record of where they may have lived or whether they had any children.

Price McNair, mentioned previously, died in 1816 prior to his parents, apparently unmarried.

Now on to Chapter three, for the next figures on our totem pole, James' and Martha's son, **John**, and his wife, **MaryAnn**.

Chapter 3 John and MaryAnn

The Knoxville Intelligencer of July 23, 1821 reported the marriage of Colonel **John McNair** to Polly Sharitz, [sic] to have taken place on the 12th of July, 1822, performed by Robert Houston, Esq. John was seventeen days shy of his thirty-ninth birthday, and Polly was just eighteen. Their first child would be born one month later.

Polly was actually MaryAnn Sherertz, born February 5, 1803, the daughter of Conrad Sherertz and MaryAnn DeVault. She was the great-granddaughter of Arnhold Sherertz, who was born in 1714 in Darmstadt, Zweibrucken, Rheinland-Pfalz, now Germany, who immigrated to Pennsylvania in 1754.

Among the passengers on the Ship Neptune, which sailed from the Port of Rotterdam, The Netherlands, and arrived in Philadelphia, PA, on September 30, 1754, were Arnhold, his wife, Catharina, and their five young sons, Jacob, Daniel, Christopher, Conrad, and John. Their sixth son, Ludwig, would be born in Pennsylvania.

For a time, the Sherertz family settled in the Southeastern Territory of Pennsylvania. Then, on June 1, 1772, Arnhold purchased several tracts of land (totaling 530 acres) on the banks of Little Connewago Creek in West Manheim Township, York County, Pennsylvania, not far from Gettysburg. It was here, in a place he called "Delight", that Arnhold built two millworks. The first was a grist and sawmill, and the second was a fulling mill, used to prepare flax into a fiber used for spinning linen.

Quoting here from the History and Folklore of Searcy Co, Arkansas, Source Book No. 1, edited by Mary Frances Harrell:

> Later John and Mary moved to the Cherokee Nation, now Bradley County, Tennessee, and in 1851 moved to Union County, Illinois, where John died the following year. Mary Ann and her children moved to Pleasant Hill, MO, to live with her son, James. The Colonel was a well-to-do farmer. He was captain of a company during the War of 1812 and some of the Indian Wars.

Actually, John and MaryAnn moved to Bradley County in 1839, (formed in February of 1836) which had *formerly* been part of the Cherokee Nation, and the purpose of the move was to take over the property left by his brother David and wife Delilah, who were now both dead, and

This building remains of the original Sherertz millworks built in 1772

whose children had been forcibly removed to the Cherokee Nation West. John and Maryann and their children appear in the 1840 and 1850 Federal census records in Bradley County, but in neither census do they have any slaves, so it is difficult to see how they operated the farm, the overland portage, and the store and tavern. The first fourteen miles of the Baltimore & Ohio railroad were opened for traffic in 1830, and now a decade later, rail traffic was beginning to reduce the freight tonnage moved on the waterways.

As for a move to Union County, Illinois, I can find no other record to support that, but I do note that Union County, *Tennessee,* was created in 1850, and was made up of land from Knox and four other counties. Court records were not kept in the new County until 1856, and much of those were destroyed in courthouse fires in 1869 and the 1870's. Therefore, I cannot definitively place the family in either location, nor have I been able to find any record of a move to Pleasant Hill, Missouri. In addition, MaryAnn was twenty years younger than John, and the next record of her is in the 1860 census, at Tomahawk, Searcy County, Arkansas, where she is listed as widowed, *but still head of household*, with four children remaining at home, three of them minors. Her son James and his family live nearby, but the widow living within his household is his mother-in-law. We will meet her (Melinda Manes), James Claiborne McNair, and his wife, Harriet (Manes), in the next chapter.

John McNair did serve in the War of 1812. This is from the National Archives:

War Of 1812
Name: John McNare
Company: BUNCH'S REG'T (1814), E. TENNESSEE MIL.
Rank - Induction: CAPTAIN
Rank - Discharge: CAPTAIN
Roll Box: 141
Roll Exct: 602
Colonel Samuel Bunch 2nd Regiment of the East Tennessee Militia.
10 Jan 1814 - 17 May 1814
CAPTAINS: James Allen, Amos Barron, Francis Berry, Andrew Breeden, Edward Buchanan, Moses Davis, Solomon Dobkins, Joseph Dunkin, John English, George Gregory, Jones Griffin, John Houk, John Howell, **John McNair**, Francis Register, Samuel Richerson, (Major) Alexander Smith, Issac Williams and Daniel Yankell .
HISTORY: Regiment of 3-month enlistees. Participated in the Battle of Horseshoe Bend; they were part of the right line of American Forces in this engagement. Provision returns indicate that there were 283 men in Bunch's Regiment at Fort Williams at the time of the Battle of Horseshoe Bend.

The Upper Creek Indians chose to support the British during the War of 1812, based in part on the resentment they felt towards the encroachment of the settlers from the East, and spurred on by the Spanish in Florida, and by Tecumseh, a Shawnee Chief, who was calling for an Indian confederation. The Upper Creek were skilled warriors, and had early successes in their efforts, including the massacre of the Garrison at Fort Mims, North of Mobile, Alabama on August 30th, 1813. The Creek's war-clubs had red painted handles, earning them the name Red Sticks among the American forces. John McNair was familiar with the ways of the Indians, and he and Andrew Cowan acted as spies for the Americans at the request of Brigadier Gen. James White. Their reports of a large contingent of Red Sticks at Horseshoe Bend on the Tallapoosa River were relayed to Major General Andrew Jackson, and a force of 3,000 men was assembled to attack them there. On March 27th, 1814, General Jackson split his forces, sending one thousand men, including

Cherokee and Lower Creek allies, down river to cross and attack from the rear, while Jackson and 2,000 men crossed up river and attacked from the front. The Red Sticks were badly outmanned by almost three to one, and lost nearly 850 of their forces, with only their leader, Chief Menawa, and about 200 of his warriors able to escape and seek refuge with the Seminoles in Florida. Upper Creek women and children, numbering about 350, were taken captive and held by the Cherokee and Lower Creeks. For the American forces, the casualties numbered forty-seven killed, and 159 wounded. One of the men wounded in the battle was a young Lieutenant named Sam Houston, who was destined to die at the Battle of the Alamo. In January of the following year, **John McNair** would serve again under General Jackson in the final event of the war, the Battle of New Orleans.

After the war, On December 2nd, 1815, John was promoted to Lieutenant Colonel, and served as Commandant of the Tennessee 10th Regiment.

And, from the United States Pension Bureau 1883 Volume 5:

In June of 1879, as the widow of a soldier, Lt. Col John McNair, who had served in the War of 1812, a pension for Mary Ann [Sherertz] McNair was established.

The list of pensioners on the rolls as of January 1st, 1883, shows that she was still receiving the pension at that time, in St. Joe, Searcy County, Arkansas, at the rate of $8.00 per month.

At some time in the past during my genealogical travels, I read a first person account that described Colonel John McNair's appearance. I can no longer find that document. I do not remember the source, or where I saw it, nor can I remember to whom the quote was attributed, but since I cannot quote directly, I offer this paraphrase, and beg your indulgence--- Colonel McNair looked so damn much like General Andrew Jackson, I thought they could be twins. And, from MaryAnn's pension application, her description of John reads thus, height 6 ft. 2 in., hair black, eyes dark gray, complexion dark. I won't add a photo of General Jackson here-but, if you look at a $20 Bill....

John McNair and MaryAnn Sherertz raised a very large family; ten children were born to them before they left Knox County and four more after their arrival in Bradley County. Here is the next generation in the family tree:

- **James Claiborne McNair** was born August 24, 1822
- Martha M. McNair was born June 6, 1823
- Myra McNair was born in 1824
- John Williams McNair was born October 31, 1825
- Price Marion McNair was born August 31, 1827
- Mary Ann Hepzibah McNair was born February 12, 1830
- Delilah McNair was born February 15, 1832
- David Howell McNair was born December 24, 1833
- Harriet Almeda McNair was born December 26, 1835
- Nicholas Nealy McNair was born July 30, 1838
- Lee Bruce McNair was born August 26, 1840
- Irena McNair was born Nov 19, 1842
- Josiah Anderson McNair was born Sep 15, 1844
- McMinnless McNair was born April 10, 1847.

As before I will deal briefly with the "aunts and uncles" of our heritage before moving on to **James Claiborne McNair** in chapter four.

Martha M. McNair married William L. Manes on August 15, 1848. They had two daughters, Mary and Melinda Jane, and six sons, John, George, David, William, Nicholas Menlus, and Williamson McNair Manes. You, the reader, will see the name Manes again. It was also spelled Manis or Maness, and is pronounced with a long "a".

Myra McNair married Alfred Davis in about 1843 in Bradley County, and I find only one daughter, Delilah Elizabeth Davis.

John Williams McNair married Median Elizabeth Johnson on October 22, 1856, in Searcy County, Arkansas and their first son, John Wriley was born there. The family then moved to South Fork, Fulton County, Arkansas where another eight children were born, named Leo Williams, Mary Elizabeth, James Marion, (who died in infancy) Median T., Laura Ida, Mattie Lu, Emma, and Eugene Franklin.

Price Marion McNair died November 9, 1840, a little over two months past his thirteenth birthday.

Mary Ann Hepzibah McNair Married James E. Carter on February 3, 1848, in Cleveland, Bradley County, Tennessee, and then moved to Missouri, where they had thirteen children.

Delilah McNair married George Elam, and they moved to Missouri where their first three children were born, named David, Elisha and Martha, before moving to Palmyra, Douglas County, Kansas, where a daughter Jennie was born.

David Howell McNair lost his life in 1862 fighting for the Confederate States during the Civil War. He was part of the Cherokee Mounted Riflemen in the 1st Reg., Cherokee Mounted Volunteers, CSA. I find it interesting that fifteen plus years after the Trail of Tears there were still many Cherokee, and their White friends, available for service during the Civil War.

Harriet Almeda McNair married John Wesley Manes, a brother of her sister Martha's husband, on January 14, 1848. This couple had nine children and Harriet died of childbirth complications less than two weeks after the last one, on April 24, 1880, at the age of forty-four. Their children were Clayborn, (not the only time the spelling will be changed) Bruce, John, George, Laura, William, Sarah, Alice and Harry Romeliss Manes.

Nicholas Nealy McNair was killed on September 20, 1863, the third and final day of the Battle of Chickamauga, Walker, Georgia, in the Civil War. He was a Sergeant in the 7th Regiment of Arkansas Infantry.

Lee Bruce McNair married a lady from Iowa named Virginia Estelle Ratliff on April 16, 1878, at Trenton, Grundy County, Missouri, and their union produced eight children, who were named Rosa Estelle, Mary, Sarah, Frank, Thomas Price, Elizabeth, and Lea Delilah McNair. Lee died on Valentines Day, February 14, 1934, at age ninety-three.

Irena McNair was near-blind for most, if not all of her life. In the 1880 Federal census for St. Joe, Searcy County, Arkansas, Irena was living with her mother, MaryAnn Sherertz McNair, who was then age seventy-seven.

Josiah Anderson McNair fought with the Confederacy for a time during the Civil War, but was captured, switched sides, and served with the Union Forces for the duration. After the war, he married Elizabeth Rainbolt, and they had two children before Josiah died in 1870. The children were Mary and Josiah McNair.

McMinnless McNair---of all the McNair names, and there are some pretty fancy ones, this one shows up with more variations than any other. He is variously listed in documents, books, and census records as McMinnless, McMinn, McMensly, MackManilus, McMenlus, and in the 1860 Searcy County census, simply as McK. His headstone in Texas, lists him as Mack. Whatever the name, he married Sarah Henderson, and had three sons and a daughter, John, Charles, Thomas and Lessie. Mr. Mc. McNair died in Avoca, Jones County, Texas on May 15, 1933, at age eighty-six.

In our next chapter, we will see that the first-born son of Colonel John McNair and MaryAnn Sherertz, **James Claiborne McNair**, was married to Harriet, whose last name was---- of course----Manes.

James Claiborne McNair and Harriet Manes
See Chapter 4

Chapter 4 James and Harriet

James Claiborne McNair married in Bradley County, Tennessee, September 14, 1848, Miss Harriet Manes. She was the sister of William and John Wesley Manes from the preceding chapter, and had three other brothers, named Pleasant Reynolds, Claiborne Lafayette, and George Manes. Her parents were George Manes of North Carolina and Melinda Lawson of Tennessee. Harriet's grandparents were Seth Manes of Bedford County, Virginia, who was a fire-breathing Methodist circuit rider, and Susan Patsy Fields, who was from Moore County, North Carolina.

James Claiborne may well have been named in honor of William Charles Cole Claiborne, who was a contemporary of Colonel John McNair, James' father. Mr. Wm. Claiborne practiced law in Sullivan County where the Colonel was born, and he was a delegate to the State constitutional convention from Sullivan County in 1796; appointed judge of the superior court in 1796; and elected as a Republican from Tennessee to the Fifth and Sixth United States Congresses, serving from November 23, 1797, to March 3, 1801. Claiborne County, Tennessee is named for him, and it looks probable that Harriet Manes' brother was also named in his honor.

While James Claiborne McNair's father was a strong military leader, the same cannot be said for the son. Quoting here, part of an article from the <u>Reminiscent History of the Ozark Region</u>, published by Goodspeed Brothers, Publishers, Chicago, 1894:

> James C. McNair spent his early days in tilling the soil, and received but little schooling. In November, 1847, he joined Company C, Fifth Tennessee Volunteer Infantry, and started for Mexico, going down the Tennessee River on a flat-boat. At Mussel Shoals the boats collided, and the men seeing their danger, jumped into the river for safety, the result being that one man was killed and one man drowned, and nothing more was ever seen of the boats. The men made their way on foot to below Florence, where they took passage on board a boat bound for Vera Cruz, which place they eventually reached. Mr. McNair was in but one engagement, and that was with guerrillas. At the end of about nine months he was discharged at Memphis, Tennessee, after which he returned home.

The above is the full extent of his military service. His three-year-younger brother, John William, enlisted, fought, and was mustered out on the same dates, which were from November 9th, 1847, to July 20th, 1848. Company C was commanded by Captain Vaughn. More will be learned of James' response to the War Between the States later in this chapter, and the devastating results of his choice.

James and Harriet had two daughters in Bradley County, but then moved the family to Searcy County, Arkansas in 1851 or early 1852, onto rich and fertile farmland near the Buffalo River at Tomahawk, and a dozen more children were to follow. Even though only eight of their brood reached adulthood, by 1894, the couple had fifty grandchildren, all living but five, and eleven great-grandchildren, all living.

James settled on 240 acres and used it for crops, but also for raising and feeding stock animals, and was quite successful in both endeavors. He became known as an expert in agricultural matters and won the admiration and respect of his peers. He served at various times as a school director, justice of the peace, and overseer of roads.

From a newspaper advertisement
as a county agricultural agent

The north-central part of Arkansas where Searcy County was located was not extensively used for growing cotton, and had a relatively small population of slaves when compared to the eastern portion of the state and to those states further east. As a consequence, when the dissolution of the Union was approaching, there was far less anti-union sentiment among the farmers of Searcy and other nearby counties. James Claiborne McNair had served briefly in the War with Mexico and he did not wish to fight again, especially in the Confederate cause. When the war broke out, he was ordered to the county seat at Burrowville (later renamed Marshall) to swear allegiance to the Confederacy. He refused and took his family into hiding in the Ozark Mountains. He would not fight against the Union, nor join them and fight against his kin and friends. James then joined with others in the Arkansas Peace Society. Here from the <u>Arkansas Historical Quarterly</u> (spring, 1958) is the situation faced by many:

> In the mountain counties of North Arkansas in the fall of 1861 secret organizations were formed for self protection and apparently to resist Confederate authority.
> Total membership in the organizations was estimated at 1700 and was concentrated in Searcy, Marion, Carroll, Izard, Fulton, and Van Buren counties. In these counties and perhaps in several others, the local units of the Arkansas Peace Society were quickly suppressed by extra-legal citizens committees acting with the county militia units and with justice of the peace courts. Many of the arrested members were forced into Confederate service either by local citizens committees or by the state military board at Little Rock. Some were tried for treason in Confederate circuit and acquitted. Many of those forced into Confederate service deserted and joined the Federal army.
> Only a part of the records relating to the Peace Society survived, but they are sufficient to show the scope and nature of the organization. Surviving documents contain the names of 240 members and suspected members. Of these 181 were located in the United States census manuscript schedules, 1860. An analysis of that record revealed that of the 181, 115 were born in Tennessee, 13 in North Carolina, and 11 in Arkansas. The leadership of the movement was also predominantly Southern-born. Six preachers among the leaders seem to have been especially influential. The brotherhood was indigenous, composed of mountaineers who had no intention of going to war on either side and who wanted to be left alone. There could of course be no neutrality, and the members were forced to take sides.

Within the documents of the Arkansas Peace Society, are listed James Claiborne McNair, along with members of other families who were, or would become, allied with the McNair clan, such as Barnett, Manes, Price, and Reeves.

I can find no record that James was ever captured or forced into service, but in 1864, he removed with his family to Missouri, returning to his Arkansas farm in 1866. The two years spent in Missouri were also two years spent in misery, because they were lived in hiding and extreme hardship, with one child stillborn and four of their other children dying there. Not all of the casualties of that terrible war were on the battlefield.

When James and Harriet were married, James became a Methodist and followed that religion for the remainder of his life, serving in various offices and as an Elder. He was at first a Whig, but early on became a Republican in his political leanings.

Let me give you the names of their fourteen children, and a line of sorrow along the way.

In Bradley County, Tennessee;
- Martha Delilah McNair was born on July 21, 1849;
- PollyAnn Malinda McNair was born January 14, 1851;

In Searcy County, Arkansas;

- Price Marion McDonald McNair was born June 25, 1852
- **And died in Missouri at age 12, Christmas Eve, 1864;**
- Thela Almeda McNair was born January 2, 1854;
- William Asbury McNair was born May 1. 1855;
- John (Jack) McNair was born January 29, 1857
- **And died in Missouri at age 7, in April 1864;**
- Harriet Susan McNair was born August 10, 1859;
- Sarah Hepzibah McNair was born June 21, 1861
- **And died in Missouri at age 3, December 31, 1864;**
- James Claiborne Washington McNair was born March 6, 1863
- **And died in Missouri at age 1, in April 1864;**
- Albert McNair **was stillborn in Missouri, March 26, 1866;**
- Ida Jane McNair was born February 4, 1868;
- John Franklin Trogdon McNair was born November 29, 1869;
- David Bruce McNair was born February 26, 1872;

- Clementine McNair was born alive on Christmas Eve, 1873
  - **but did not survive the day.**
  -

Six of fourteen who died so young; is a century and a half later too late to shed a tear or light a candle?

Chapter 5 will feature **David Bruce McNair**, but first a little about his siblings who survived to adulthood.

Martha Delilah McNair married Benjamin Franklin Henley in 1866, in Searcy County, Arkansas. To this union were added nine children, named James Alfred, William Lafayette, Jackson Franklin, Harriet, Green B., Mattie D., Blaine, Benjamin and John Henley.

Perhaps this is a good time to reflect a little about names. Throughout this book are scattered names that will surely sound oddly familiar, and some that will simply sound odd. Jackson, Franklin, Lafayette, Claiborne, Washington, and Madison, were patriots and heroes, national figures; patriotic fervor attached many of their names to the children of pioneering families. Other names were biblical, at least originally, like Daniel, James, John and Matthew, or Mary, Martha and Delilah, and the odd sounding Hepzibah, which is a Hebrew name which means "my *delight* is in her." Perhaps Arnhold Sherertz could have named his Pennsylvania millworks property Hepzibah. I will not be covering the full Manes family tree in this book, but must include here the biblical names of Manes triplets born in 1770, in North Carolina --- Shadrack, Meshach, and Abednego.

Pollyann Malinda McNair married George Napoleon Rainbolt on September 9, 1869, in Searcy County. They had nine children, John William, Martha, Hepzibah Sarah, Isaac Lafayette, Frances Almeda, James, Eliza, Estella Tennessee, and Marcus Rainbolt. In the 1900 Searcy County census, Irena, James Claiborne's near-blind sister was living with this family, because her mother, MaryAnn Sherertz McNair had died in May of 1894, at age 91. In chapter 5, we will see the blind Irena involved in a child's tragic death.

Thela Almeda McNair married Lewis Quinton Thompson, a physician, and they had a son and two daughters, Lewis, Eudocia Belle, and Harriette Ellen before leaving Arkansas. Their last daughter, Mabel was born in Gridley, Butte County, California.

William Asbury McNair married Rhoda Francis Rainbolt about 1876 in Searcy County. They had twelve children, Britomarte, (I like the name, and hope it is from the Faerie Queene, and not Britomarte the Man Hater, of Civil War fame.) Albert, Martha Delilah, Rosa, Melinda, Jennie Mae, William, Bruce Napoleon, Jack Franklin, James, Agnes, (Aggie) and Troy David McNair.

Harriet Susan McNair married Solomon Clinton Pruitt on October 22, 1874. Twelve children were born to them, named Mary Eudocia, Thela Ann, James, Harriett, George, David, Gertrude, Martha Jane, John, Nancy, Blaine Roberta, and Sibyl Clara Pruitt. Chapter six will bring the marriage of David Cleborn McNair to Sibyl Gertrude Barnett. Harriet Susan McNair is Sibyl's grandmother. Harriet's brother, David Bruce McNair, (chapter five) is David Cleborn McNair's father, making David Cleborn and Sibyl first cousins, once removed. (One generation separates them, with Harriet Susan McNair as their common ancestor.)

Ida Jane McNair married Dr. William F. Rogers on March 15, 1888, and had five daughters and a son. They were Settie, Alice, Martha, William, Inez, and Dora. In the 1900 census, Dr. Rogers is listed as a Physician and Surgeon, but by 1920, he is listed as a merchant of retail groceries.

John Franklin Trogdon McNair married twice. First to Louella Williams in June of 1890, having two daughters and two sons, Mary Vina, Harriet, James Claiborn, (no "e" on the end) and Valentine. His second marriage in 1918 was to Minnie Ann Lewis, with eight more children, named Laura, Leon, Wanda, a son Beecher, Minnie, John, Pearl, and Muriel McNair.

Now on to **David Bruce McNair**, the last of the children born to James Claiborne and Harriet able to survive to adulthood.

Chapter 5 David Bruce and Sarah

David Bruce McNair married a southern belle named Sarah Elizabeth Kester, on November 22, 1894, when he was 22, and his bride was just two months past her 16th birthday, she having been born September 22, 1878.

Sarah's father was Isaac Wilson Kester. According to Ellen Harriet (McNair) Barley, one of David and Sarah's daughters, Isaac Wilson Kester died seven months shy of his forty-third birthday, of pneumonia, after having swum his horse across an icy river during a bear hunt. Engaged in the Civil War, Isaac fought on the Union side, in Company M. of the 2nd Regiment, Arkansas Calvary Volunteers. His pneumonia death on February 11, 1882, left his widow, Sinia Louisa (Price) Kester with a very small war pension, and seven children under the age of fifteen. Sinia Louisa Price had also lost her father, William, and two of her brothers, Lindsay William and Charles William Price, during the Civil War.

Sinia Louisa Price's father John William (Buck) Price, born in 1800, was married to Elizabeth Lindsay, and both of them were from North Carolina, as shown in the 1850 and 1860 census records for Arkansas. Martha Price, of chapter 2 was also born in North Carolina (in 1753) but I can find no records that tie these two Price families together. Nor can I find any link tying either family to the famous Confederate General, Sterling Price, who was born in 1809 in Prince Edward County, Virginia.

David Bruce McNair was the thirteenth child in a family of fourteen, and so he already had four nephews by his two oldest sisters on the day he was born. His Mother turned forty and his father fifty in that same year.

The 1900 Arkansas census shows David, Sarah, and their first three children living in St. Joe Township, while the 1910 census lists the family as having moved to Tomahawk Township. Both townships are in Searcy County, and in both locations David Bruce is listed as owning his farm and land free and clear of any mortgages. In 1940, the family is in Bruno, part of Hampton Township, in Marion County; a different County, but just a hop, skip, and a jump from St. Joe, or Tomahawk.

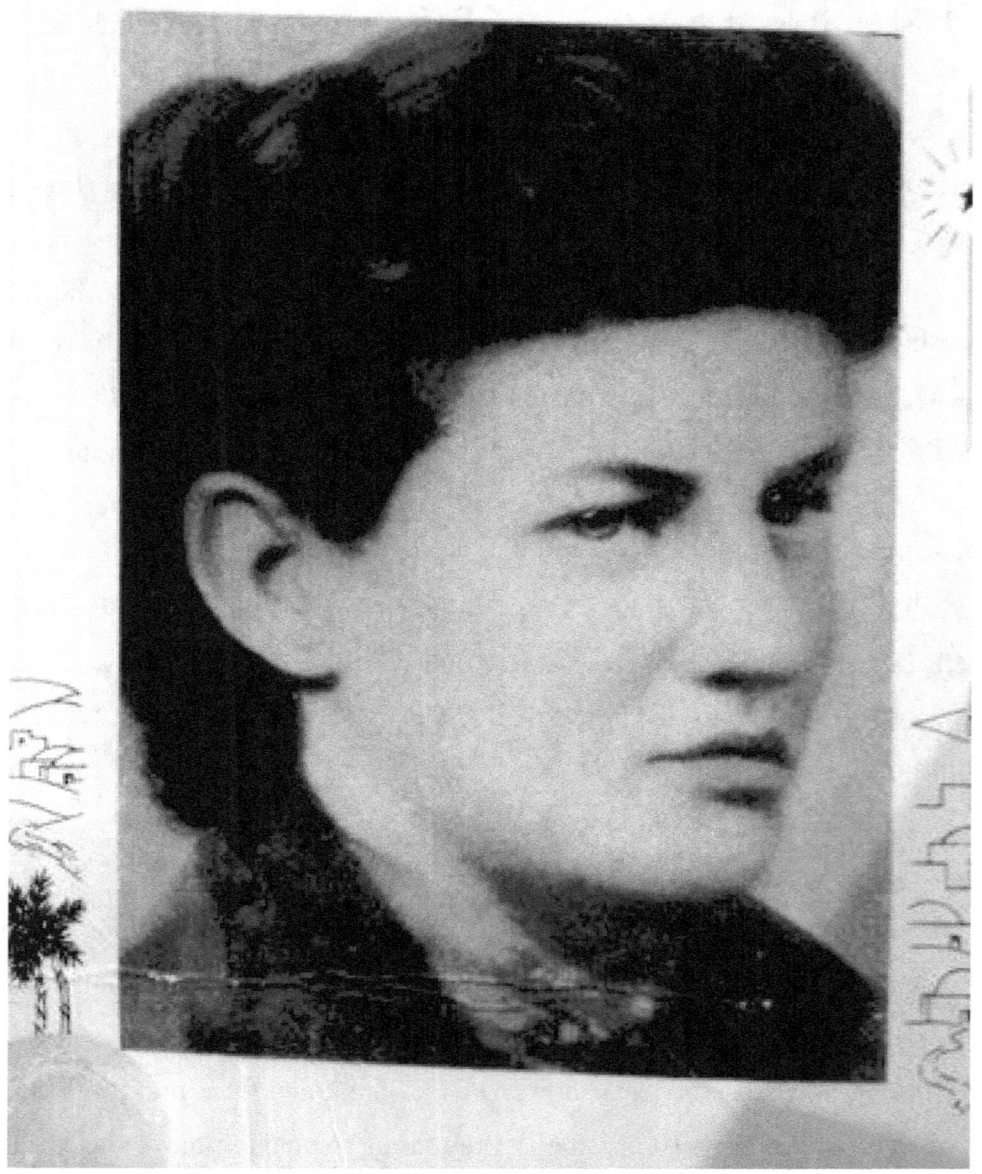

Sarah Elizabeth Kester at age 16

Sarah in her eighties
We should all be so wrinkle free!

Sinia Louisa (Price) Kester

Purported to be Isaac Wilson Kester, apparently posed in a photo studio cutout

The 1910 census also reveals a sad story; Sarah is shown as having had seven children but only six are living. Hue Kester McNair had been born August 20, 1902, and while still an infant in his cradle, was placed near the fireplace hearth for warmth. Visiting from her nearby home with George Rainbolt was David Bruce's aunt, Irena McNair, the near-blind younger sister of James Claiborne McNair. Irena was attempting to remove a kettle of boiling water from the fireplace and accidentally spilled it, scalding baby Hue to death. This infant was the only one of Bruce and Sarah's eleven children who did not live to adulthood.

One note here about the name David Bruce. In the first census where he is listed, at age eight in 1880, his name is shown as David B. McNair. The census taken in 1890 was lost to a fire, so there is no record, and in 1900, James Claiborne's family is listed as if every child was still at home, even though all of them had married and left home from six to as much as thirty-five years earlier. In that household, he is once again listed as David B. McNair. The very next entry, on the same page of the census, lists him as Bruce D., married to Sarah, with the first few of their children. The 1910 and 1930 censuses also list him as Bruce, and the family was missed in the 1920 census. The 1940 census lists him as David B., and interestingly, he is noted as the person supplying the answers to the census-taker. No birth certificate is available, and while his given name was probably David Bruce, his own choice seems to have been the reverse, so I favor letting Shakespeare's Juliet make the call; "What's in a name? That which we call a rose, by any other name would smell as sweet."

You may recall back in chapter one, that Daniel McNair got a little intoxicated and ended up insulting the King's Attorney in court, so you may be able to appreciate that what happened to David Bruce in 1909-1910, was surely no more than his unknowing attempt to keep alive a little family tradition. I like to call this story:

Grandpa goes a-courtin' (Supreme that is)

ARKANSAS SUPREME COURT 1910 SESSION
Hancock V. State. Opinion delivered December 12, 1910. 1. L1quors-Solicit1ng Orders In Prohibition Terr1tory-C1rculars.-An indictment which charges the defendant with having violated the act of April 1, 1907, making it unlawful to solicit orders for the sale of liquors in prohibition territory, by sending into

prohibition territory "a circular in the form of a memorandum book" containing certain advertising matter which is set forth, and thereby soliciting orders for the sale of intoxicating liquors, alleges a violation of the statute. (Page 41.)

2. Statute-Construction.-The terms of a statute are to be construed according to their usually accepted meaning in common language. (Page 43)

Appeal from Searcy Circuit Court; Brice B. Hudgins, Judge; affirmed.

STATEMENT BY THE COURT.

The indictment, omitting formal parts, is as follows: "That the said F. M. Hancock, in the county of Searcy, and the State of Arkansas, on the 10th day of December, A. D. 1909, being then and there a licensed liquor dealer in the city of Eureka Springs, Arkansas, unlawfully did solicit orders for intoxicating liquors in territory of this State, in which territory it would be unlawful to make sales of intoxicating liquors, to wit: in Tomahawk Township, Searcy County, Arkansas, by then and there sending into said prohibition territory certain advertising matter soliciting orders for the sale of intoxicating liquors by express, the said advertising matter being a circular in the form of a memorandum book, containing the following advertising matter, soliciting orders for the sale of intoxicating liquors, to wit:

'The Frisco Saloon, Hancock & Long, Props., Oldest Reliable Liquor House in North Arkansas, Wholesale and Retail Wine and Liquor Dealers. All Goods Bought in Bond. No Cheap Blend or Rectified Stuff. We handle all the leading brands. No goods sold to minors. Pick out what you want, and send us your nearest merchant's check, money order or cash, and goods will go out on next train. Freight or express goes every day in the week. Anything you want not on the list write for information to Hancock & Long, Box 142, Eureka Springs, Arkansas. Price list on the inside. Address orders to F. M. Hancock, Box 142, Eureka Springs, Arkansas.' (Here prices of liquors, for one gallon and half gallon quantities, is set out in the indictment. With $1.50 rebate for empties). 'Will box and ship anything you want. Jugs or bottled goods. Strictly cash house. Telegram, 'phone and credit orders will not be filled to any one. Hancock & Long, Box 142, Eureka Springs, Arkansas. Things to remember. Knowing very well that publicity is not desired by many who purchase whisky, we desire to point out to you why you should be one of our customers. For the past few years several firms in large cities have carried on an advertising campaign, and, in order to pay for it, they are obliged to make their goods of an inferior grade. We are not going in this business on so large a scale, but only desire to secure our share of the business in this section, and in doing this we are going to give our customers goods that are right, and not the kind that is sold cheap and consists of impure ingredients. When you make one purchase from us, we feel satisfied that we can add you to our list, which now contains many of the names of the most prominent men in this section. The goods are pure, and, if you find that they are not as represented, ship them back at our expense, because we are desirous of having pleased patrons. We are located near the famous Basin Spring, and when in Eureka Springs we invite you to make our place your headquarters. "Right treatment to all, and goods at the right price" is our motto. We hope to add you to

58

our patrons, but, in case you do not desire anything in our line, kindly hand this to a friend, who you think will be interested. Enclosed you will find our new price list, which is not subject to any change in price. Thanking you in advance for a future order, we beg to remain, " 'Very respectfully," 'Hancock & Long, "'Proprietors Frisco Saloon.'

"Which said advertising matter was sent by express by the said F. M. Hancock from Eureka Springs, Carroll County, Arkansas, in a package, containing a shipment of liquor, to one **Bruce McNair**, and shipped by express and delivered to him, the said **Bruce McNair**, at Gilbert, in Tomahawk Township, Searcy County, Arkansas, which said last-named place is in territory wherein the sale of intoxicating liquors is unlawful. Against the peace and dignity of the State of Arkansas."

A demurrer in short was filed to this indictment, and the same was overruled, and exceptions were saved. The case was submitted to the court, sitting as a jury, upon the following testimony:

It was agreed that the appellant was a licensed liquor dealer in Eureka Springs, in the State of Arkansas, and that Tomahawk Township, in Searcy County, Arkansas, is a prohibition district.

Bruce McNair was introduced as a witness, and identified a certain memorandum book, which was introduced in evidence. This memorandum book contains the language set up in the indictment, and there is no contention that there is any variance between the allegations and the proof. The witness testified that he received this memorandum book in Tomahawk Township, Searcy County, Arkansas, the latter part of the year 1909; that is, in November, 1909. That the same came by express, together with a package of alcohol, which had been shipped him by the appellant. The court found the appellant guilty, and assessed his punishment at a fine of two hundred ($200.00) dollars. Motions for a new trial and in arrest of judgment were filed, which were overruled, and exceptions were saved.

The case that was being appealed to the State Supreme Court was that of the liquor dealer, and I have not been able to find whether or not Bruce McNair was ever charged or found guilty of possessing the "devil's brew" in a prohibition district, but I do know that the Supreme Court was located in Little Rock, which was *not* in a prohibition district, and my guess is that if Bruce had to take the train that far, he may well have decided to not come home with an empty rucksack. Just a guess, mind you.

David Bruce and Sarah Elizabeth McNair had eleven children of whom ten survived to adulthood. They were:

- James William Price McNair was born December 5, 1895;
- Ida L. McNair was born September 21, 1897;

- Telia Irene McNair was born March 6, 1900;
- Hue Kester McNair was born August 20, 1902 died June 22, 1903;
- Raymond Bruce McNair was born October 10, 1904;
- Webster Dow McNair was born November 16, 1906;
- **David Cleborn McNair** was born June 19, 1909;
- Lee Joseph McNair was born October 8, 1911;
- Sarah Elizabeth "Beth" McNair was born March 26, 1914;
- Alford Wilson "Billy" McNair was born September 18, 1916;
- Ellen Harriet McNair was born April 3, 1919.

David Bruce McNair died September 12, 1964 at Harrison, Boone County, Arkansas, and Sarah Elizabeth Kester McNair died March 7, 1971, also at Harrison, both having reached the age of ninety-two.

Chapter 6 will highlight **David Cleborn McNair**, but first a little on his siblings.

James William Price McNair was "Uncle Jim" to my brothers and me. His registration papers for WWI described him as tall, of medium build, and with blue eyes and red hair. He married Leona Adams in 1914 and they had three children, being Edna in 1916, who married Fred Mysinger, and Demoi in 1920, who married George Sissom and moved to Kansas. Finally, Hoyt James McNair in 1925, who married Joyce Sasser and had sons Larry and Ralph.

Aunt Ida McNair married Ray Courtney in 1922, and they had at least one child, named Elihu McNair Courtney in 1923.

Aunt Irene married John Wyatt Strunk in 1917 or 1918. I am not aware of any children born to them. The 1930 census list Wyatt J. Strunk and Telia living in Tulsa, Oklahoma, where he is a traveling salesman of groceries. Ten years earlier, his occupation was the same, but they were living in Monett, Missouri. Irene died in Harrison, Arkansas in January 1987, at age eighty-six.

Uncle Raymond moved to Fort Worth, Texas, where he met, and in 1929, married, a Texas born nineteen year old named Faye Havins. On August 19, 1930, a daughter was born, named Quinda Faye McNair. Raymond was working then as a clerk for an oil company. Raymond soon moved into work for the federal government, and was the Chief of the Records Management Section at the Bureau of the Census for the 1950 U.S. Census. He also presided over the Records Management Division of the Public Health Service, and the Internal Revenue Service in

Washington, D.C. After his retirement from the Federal Government, Raymond served as mayor of Sunrise Beach, Texas, for a number of years.

Webster "Uncle Web" Dow McNair married Dottie Theresa Glenn on August 11, 1932 at Olvey, Boone County, Arkansas. Dottie was born January 6, 1910 in Eros, Marion County, Arkansas, and died December 31, 1987, in Texas, while Webster survived her by almost two years, dying at age eighty-three, on Christmas day, 1989, in Winfield, Kansas, near his little sister, Ellen. Web and Dottie spent most of their lives in Trona, California, a Mojave Desert town noted for blistering summer temperatures that often reached 110-115 degrees. Web made his career at American Potash and Chemical Corp.

In the late 1930's and early 1940's, there was a train that passed through Trona during the night, and Web and Dottie lived nearby. One morning however, the train was late, and there was a little boy and girl out playing near the track. The boy decided it would be fun to hold a stick on the track and watch the train run over it. The engineer thought at first he was seeing tumbleweeds near the track, and when he realized they were children, he stopped the train, but not before the footstep on the engine hit the boy in the head, fracturing his skull. Webster rushed to the boy's aid and took him to the hospital, where he recovered after a few days. News reports later said that not only did the railroad company pay for the hospital bills, but also gave the boy's family *one hundred dollars*, part of which his mother used to buy the boy a suit and hat. My, how times have changed!

Uncle Lee McNair married Zelma Nina Pennington on September 15, 1939 and they had three sons and two daughters, named Gary Lee, Kenneth W., Boyd Leslie, Joyce K., and Gayle E. McNair.

Sarah Elizabeth "Aunt Beth" McNair married Clarence S. Williams when she was twenty, on August 21, 1934, and they lived in Harrison, Arkansas. Their daughter, Agnes Irene, was born on the same day as my brother John Rupert McNair, July 2, 1935. Martha Susan was born on November 11, 1948, and son Kirby was born in about 1950.

Alfred Wilson McNair was "Uncle Billy", and he married Clarice Sasser on February 8, 1939, when she was just five months past her sixteenth birthday. Their children were Barbara Ellen, Robert Len, and Teresa Jo McNair.

Aunt Ellen Harriet McNair graduated from Bruno High School and then Wichita Business College in Kansas. In Wichita, she married Bernard B. Barley, a Kansas native, on September 6, 1946. The couple had two sons, Bruce and Alan. Ellen was an aspiring poet, and belonged to the Midwest Chaparral Poetry Society and the Kansas Authors Club. Mr. Barley passed away on January 31, 1977, and on February 16, 1991, Ellen remarried, to Erwin L. Harris. He died July 22, 1999, and Ellen died on April 15, 2000, at the age of eighty-one.

Now on to **David Cleborn McNair** in chapter 6.

Chapter 6 David and Sibyl, *and* David and Kathryn

David Cleborn McNair was the seventh child, and the fifth of seven sons born to Bruce and Sarah McNair. We cannot learn why his middle name is spelled so unlike his grandfather's Claiborne as it is, but can only say that while the intent is clear, the spelling "ain't" so near. By the time of his birth, only one grandparent was alive, that being Sinia Louisa Price Kester. Even though his paternal grandfather, James Claiborne, had lived to the ripe old age of eighty-four, he was still two years dead before David was even born. That is the nature of the generational gaps of very large families that were so common in the eighteenth and nineteenth centuries in rural, agricultural based America.

David and his siblings would be the first generation of our McNair family to be born into a farming lifestyle and then leave it en masse.

With the exception of Fayetteville, education in the Ozarks was traditionally well behind the majority of the nation, and to many in this very rural area, education was almost considered a threat to their way of life. Schooling beyond the eighth grade was simply considered unnecessary to the agricultural community, and advanced education might tempt the youngsters away from the farm. Additionally, funding for schools and teachers was limited in the days following WWI. Nevertheless, there developed enough pressure in Marion County for better schools that the Bruno School District was created by Act #278 of the 1920 legislature, and in the fall of 1921 a four year High School was opened in a cement block building. The federal Smith-Hughes Act of 1917 had created vocational education opportunities, particularly in vocational agriculture, and the Bruno High School took advantage of the minimal funding provided to create an agricultural curriculum. A young man named J.B. Ewart, was hired to provide those classes at about the time that David McNair was starting High School. Mr. Ewart created the Lincoln Aggie Club, (Future Farmers of America) the first of its kind in the nation, and David was a member.

Now, as my brothers and I can surely tell you, when *we* were young we had to walk to school and back, barefoot, in knee-deep snow, uphill both ways, *but even we* did not have to design and build our own gymnasium. David and a couple of his brothers, however, did just that. Previously, all the basketball games were played on an outdoor court, but Mr. Ewart and the Smith-Hughes Aggie boys rallied the community, having them haul gravel and sand, while the

Aggie boys provided the labor to build a cobblestone gymnasium. To the left of the door to this gym is a marble slab which reads:

AGGIE HALL   1926
Plans and specifications by the Smith-Hughes Aggie boys
and erected under their supervision.

A marble slab on the right side names J. B. Ewart, instructor, and the boys who worked forty hours or more on the construction: Earl Adams, Pierce Adams, Everett Burnes, Frank Burnes, Fred Burnes, Lester Burnes, Hugh Elam, Paul Elam, Garnett Elton, Howard Keeling, H. S. Keeling, Roy Keeling, **David McNair, Webster McNair, Raymond McNair**, Dolph Milligan, Hobart Milligan, Jerome Morris, Hoyt Pyle, Norvel Pyle, Rudolph Setzler, Alvard Swafford, Gales Swafford, Howard Wilson, Hugh Wilson, and Woodrow Wilson.

Aggie Hall, on County Rd. 9 in Bruno is now on the National Register of Historic Places. The gym allowed the boys to hone their basketball skills, and in his senior year, David and his teammates on the Bruno High School boys' basketball team won the Arkansas State Championship in their division. David's basketball skills were so good that he may have been (unproven) offered an athletic scholarship to the University of Oklahoma. He chose not to accept the scholarship, and my brother Michael says he believes that was a decision Dad regretted deeply for the rest of his life.

The cobblestone building was a God-send in December of 1928, when the main school building was burned out. This was on a Friday and the citizenry rallied once again, partitioning off four classrooms in the gym, plus adding woodstoves and flues, working around the clock so that classes could resume on Monday morning. New construction followed and a new four room schoolhouse was completed in 1929.

Aggie Hall in Bruno, Marion Co., Arkansas

David grew up on a farm, and always kept a spot in his heart for the farming way of life, although he felt no great compunction to soil his own hands but rather to raise a family full of boys that might hoe and plant and weed and irrigate and harvest the crops as best they could. Perhaps the term "gentleman farmer" would be best employed. The first three of his sons were born in Arkansas, the fourth in Kansas, and the fifth in Colorado, and we will learn a little about each of them in this chapter. In late 1940 or early 1941, David and wife Sibyl uprooted from the Arkansas Ozarks and with three sons in tow moved to the Wichita, Kansas area. The Wichita City Directory for 1943 lists David and family living at 645 Gow St., and lists his occupation as Manager for the Kansas Geological Survey. None of my older brothers remember him in that occupation but even though his education was in agriculture, he was also very adept at dealing with people, and that is the essence of managerial skills, so in choosing whether the City Directory information was a misprint, or he indeed had that job, I vote for him being able to handle that job with pure aplomb. (just before publication I found some ancient tax returns that verified that job)

His next work was as an Insurance Agent for Farmers and Bankers Life Insurance, and he stayed with that company, elevated to General (manager) Agent when he moved to Colorado in 1945. On May 16, 1944, David was drafted into the Army at Fort Leavenworth, Kansas during WWII. His wife, Sibyl Barnett, was left behind to care for four sons alone, aged three to twelve, and she was so overwhelmed by that to the point of a nervous breakdown, severe enough to require hospitalization. David applied for a hardship discharge to be able to return home and care for his sons, but it took a long time for that discharge to come through on the 89th day of the enlistment. (One day longer and he would have been eligible for VA benefits, which he never received.) The four boys were placed in the Kansas Children's home, the younger two briefly until their dad's sister, Irene, and her husband John Strunk took them into their home. The older sons, Norman and John remained in the home until David was finally able to arrange a divorce and new marriage, being the only way that the State of Kansas would release them into his custody, on September 23, 1945.

David Cleborn McNair was married twice, and we will deal with the ancestry of each of his wives fully in separate chapters, as they bring plenty of diversity to the party.

Sibyl Gertrude Barnett (see chapter seven) was David Cleborn's first wife, marrying on July 19th, 1931. She was the daughter of David Jackson Barnett, a high school teacher in Tomahawk, and his wife Gertrude Pruitt. The Great Depression was in full swing, with little hope of better times to come. The couple had four sons and we will learn a little about them here.

Norman David McNair

Norman David McNair was the first-born son of David and Sibyl. Norman was born in St. Joe, Arkansas, in the Easter season, on April 24th, 1932 in the home of his parents, nine months and five days after their marriage. Norman grew to be tall and lean, and was imbued with an amazing talent for art, especially woodcarving, and a deep and abiding faith in his own ability and capability for succeeding in the tasks he chose to undertake. His woodcarvings were done rapidly, and exhibited a forceful and striking, almost primitive, stylization that made them a pleasure to see and touch.

His early adulthood was interrupted by the Korean War when he served his country by enlisting in the Navy. He had a desire to become a Doctor, but the closest he came to that goal was assignment as a corpsman in the Navy, serving first in the Korean Theater, and ending his service assigned to supervise a hospital ward at the San Diego Naval Station. He was discharged honorably in December of 1952. He worked for some time as a research chemist for Chevron, in their Ortho Division. In a 1960 *Journal of the American Chemistry Society* (JACS) article titled *"Ion Transport in Sodium-Ammonia Solutions" by J. L. Dye , R. F. Sankuer ,and G. E. Smith*, Norman D. McNair is recognized for his assistance in conducting the experimental work.

Norman also later worked in the taxi and limousine business as both driver and dispatcher. Norman had a wicked sharp wit and sense of humor, was an avid Bridge player and was a well above average bowler and pool player.

Norman David McNair married **Shirley Claire Grady**, the first-born daughter of Hawthorne (Hoff) Grady and his wife Carmel E. Tobin. The marriage took place on October 4, 1952. Shirley was a third generation native-born Californian, but here I will slide back two additional generations, to her great-grandfather, the original Irish immigrant, and a true California "Forty-Niner". According to census records, he was born in about 1822, and his wife in about 1828. I have been unable to determine when James Henry Grady and his future bride, Mary Dolly, left Tuam, Galway, Ireland, or at what port they arrived in America, but on November 11th, 1847, they were married in St. Patrick's Catholic Church in New Orleans, Louisiana. In 1849 they boarded ship, and sailed for the gold fields of California. It is believed they took land portage across the Isthmus of Panama, (the Panama Canal was still more than sixty years distant) rather than sailing the additional 8,000 miles around Cape Horn at the southern tip of South America.

In San Francisco James established an enterprise in the clothing business, an occupation he had practiced before coming to California, but the great fire of 1851 damaged commerce so badly that he took his wife and year old son and moved to Tuolumne County to pursue his fortune as a miner. Mr. Grady apparently enjoyed success and continued in mining because twenty years later, James, with his wife and eight children, including a set of seven year old twins, is shown in the US Census, in San Francisco, and his occupation is still listed as miner. According to his son Theodore, (Shirley's grandfather) James Henry Grady's death occurred as a result of being run over by cars in Virginia City, Nevada in 1874. Theodore's statement did not elaborate on the term "cars," leaving this researcher wondering. Perhaps railroad cars, but would he not have said "hit by a train"? Perhaps something horse-drawn, but wouldn't that be a cart, a carriage, or wagon? My conclusion finally, and only my best guess, is that since James Henry was a miner, he may have died in a mining accident, being run over by the specialized railcars used to move silver and gold ore out of the underground mining shafts in and around the Comstock Lode.. A tragedy in any event, to lose so young, at age fifty-two, the proud and adventurous Irish progenitor of the Grady clan in California.

James and Mary Grady had nine children; the first was his father's namesake, James Henry, born in New Orleans, but he tragically died within two hours of his birth. The remaining 8 children were born in California, and their names were James Thomas, John Henry, Kate Francis, Molly Helen, Robert Emmit, Theodore, born October 29, 1860, Edron Joseph, and Emma. Theodore was stricken with scarlet fever when just an infant, and as a result, became, in his own words, "halfway, semi-deaf". In spite of that optimistic description, his deafness was profound enough that he was enrolled in the Deaf Institute in Berkeley, California. Here, from the Centennial Senior Yearbook of the Deaf Institute Berkeley (1860-1960) courtesy of Joyce Ingraham:

Theodore Grady was born in a Tuolumne Mining Camp, October 29, 1860. He became deaf at the age of 3 and entered the Berkeley School (for the deaf) in January 1870. After finishing school he entered the University of California, graduating in May 1883. He was Deputy Tax Collector of San Francisco for two years. He entered Johns Hopkins University in 1886 as a graduate student in psychology and pedagogy. (The art of teaching) He was appointed a teacher in our school in 1887. He entered the Law School of U.C. in 1895, and was admitted to the Bar in 1897. While still holding his position as teacher, he was connected with a large law firm in San Francisco.

The California School for the Deaf is now located in Fremont, California, and has a residence named Grady Hall. This high school boys' residence is named for Theodore Grady, the first deaf person to earn a degree at the University of California, and later one of the first deaf

69

lawyers in the state of California. Clearly, Theodore's disability was well overcome by a brilliant mind and a diligent and compelling work ethic. The woman he was to marry, on July 25, 1889, was also a pupil at the Deaf Institute, and as she was eight years younger than he, may have had some of her classes from him. Her name was May Grace Kiddell. She was born January 18, 1868, in Missouri, to John Frank Kiddell (born in England) and his wife, Harriet (Hattie) Wilcox. (Born in Canada) In a special supplement to the 1890 US Census, May Kiddell lists the cause of her deafness as spinal meningitis at the age of five. The marriage of Theodore and May also produced a large family, of eight children, whose names were Chancellor, Theodore Jr., Dwight, Genevieve, Madeline, Viola, Hawthorne (Hoff), and Elwood. In this list of children, Viola had the middle name Fishbourn, while apparently the other seven had the middle name Kiddell. To a student of genealogy, that Fishbourn name is like a big red cape to a bull, and I will not be surprised if future research happens to turn up that name in the lineage of one of May Kiddell's parents.

Hoff Grady was the seventh child, born shortly before Christmas, on December 21, 1902. In 1929, he married Carmel Tobin, an Irish lass with a touch of German as well. Carmel was the daughter of Michael Joseph Tobin, born in New York on February 28, 1868 to James Tobin and Alice Meagher, both of Ireland. Carmel's mother was Mary Theresa (Hannah) Burkhardt, born October 12, 1869 in San Francisco, to Fred Burkhardt of Württemberg, Germany, and his wife, Hannah Fox of Ireland. Carmel's father, Michael J. Tobin, began work as a shipping clerk and bookkeeper for a wholesale cigar company, but retired after a long career as an accountant for the University of California at Berkeley. Before beginning a family, Hoff and Carmel bought a home at 1046 Ventura in Albany, California. Hoff was working for the Federal Government as a Traffic Foreman. Their first of three daughters, Shirley Claire Grady, was born April 13, 1933, followed by Carol Ann on January 21, 1936 and Joan Theresa on February 8, 1938. Their fourth child, a son, was Kenneth Edwin Grady, born June 8, 1941.

Norman and Shirley were blessed with four daughters, namely Norma Diane in 1953, Sharon Kaye in 1954, Deloris Elaine in 1957, and Catherine in 1959. Catherine gave them a granddaughter in 1986 named Rebecca Carmel Lynn. Norman and Shirley were divorced in 1969. Norman passed away July 28, 1992 and Shirley died January 20, 2009.

John Rupert McNair

The second son born to David and Sibyl, on July 2nd, 1935, was **John Rupert McNair**. John, like his brother Norman, was born in the home at Saint Joe and would be the last child to be born in that locale, perhaps in part because of the Barnett-Henley feud. The Barnett-Henley feud (see chapter 7) had lessened in intensity, but had not gone away, and since David's wife was a Barnett, David automatically became a target of the Henley wrath. I do not know when it occurred, but on one occasion David received a fist from behind, to the side of his head, that knocked him out cold. After he was blind-sided, Sibyl's brother Joe went hunting for the fellow who had done the deed, and gave him a beating. At some point after this incident, David and Sibyl and their two sons moved to Harrison, in Boone County, Arkansas, leaving the feud behind for good.

John Rupert McNair started life as an Ozark farm boy, but was destined for a life far from the farm and far from mundane. He was born on July 2, 1935 in time for the Independence Day festivities, in the same shotgun-cabin as his older brother had been, in St. Joe, Arkansas.

Before his next brother is born, the moving began, partially due to the feud, but also because his father had tried his hand at farming with less than stellar success. The crops were poor, the cow didn't give adequately of its potential bounty, and the Great Depression became more, far more, than just that "Wall Street Thing." The family moved first to Harrison for a time and then on to Wichita, Kansas in search of better times. In 1945 David C., now with four sons, and a new wife, moved to Pueblo, Colorado and its environs. After arrival there, shorter but still disruptive moves continued; first to 2111 Pine St., then a place on 13th St., to a small farm in unincorporated Blende, to a mountain cabin at the foot of the Rockies in Beulah, back to Pueblo at 306 Reservoir Dr., and then to the B&B Court Motel on Lake St., waiting for completion of construction of a small, but new, home; so finally settling at 3041 O'Neal on the west side of Pueblo in 1953. All of those moves were made in a little over seven years and must have been pretty disruptive to young scholars just hoping to return to the same school of the preceding year's studies. Nevertheless, John graduated from Central High School in 1954, and received an AA degree from Pueblo Junior College in 1956. John then left home and attended Colorado State University in Fort Collins and was awarded a Bachelor of Science in Fisheries Management in 1958.

In August of that year John entered the U.S. Army, training in Fort Ord, California, before being assigned to the Seventh Army near Frankfurt in Hanau, Germany. There John was a teacher of General Education for the troops and for a number of months ran the Armed Forces Institute. Taking advantage of leave time, long weekends, and free flights using hops on military aircraft John was able to travel extensively, and managed trips to Athens, Copenhagen, Paris, London, and Edinburgh. One of his hops in 1960 took him to Adana, Turkey, where he found a rather cold reception, (as was given any Americans at the time) because he arrived not long after Francis Gary Powers had been shot down in his U-2 spy plane over Sverdlosk in the then USSR. Nikita Kruschev was threatening strikes against U-2 locations, and Adana was among those sites. John also toured the Rhine River in Germany by boat.

When he had completed his military duty he returned home for a short period and then, in January of 1961, he moved to Boulder, Colorado. Surrounding these periods of time John spent four summers employed as a fisheries biologist on Kodiak Island, Alaska, for the US Fish and Wildlife Department in 1957, 1958, 1960 and 1961. In Boulder he returned to his studies, changing his major to English. I remember him telling me at some point that he loved fishing and the outdoor life so much that he worried he might spoil it by continuing to make it his vocation, and that he had gained an appreciation for teaching while in the Army in Germany; thus the change in his focus at the University of Colorado at Boulder. From 1965 to 1967 he worked as the City-County Health Inspector, and followed that with two years teaching science at Rishel Junior High School in a Denver suburb. For five years during this period John was married to Evelyn Sigismonde, but had no children. On September 27, 1968 John married a second time, to Anne Marie Haskins of Fort Walton Beach, Florida, and this union produced two children; John Rupert Jr. in 1969, who married Andrea Szekely, who was born in Santa Monica, California on December 31st, 1973, and Michael Evan in 1977, both in Boulder. John married for a third time on May 19, 1998 to Susan Fenyves of New York.

He continued with post-graduate work and in 1977 was awarded a PhD in English from the University of Colorado, and was accepted as an Assistant Professor of English Literature at the University of North Carolina in Charlotte. During his time there he escorted groups of his students to Stratford and London for eight summers of a three week Shakespeare course with emphasis on performance, including that of the students. He continued in his position until his retirement, as Associate Professor Emeritus in 2003. Over the course of many years he has also pursued an independent trade in old, sometimes rare, books, maps, manuscripts, art, and ephemera, buying, selling, and collecting, and along the way developing expertise in restoration, hand coloring, appraisal, and even bookbinding. He has authored and co-authored numerous technical articles on various subjects., including in the *American Journal of Criminal Justice, Volume 7, Number 2*, an article entitled *Integrating the study of criminal justice and literature* by J. David Hirschel and John R. McNair, and in the *Children's Literature Association Quarterly Volume 11, Number 4*, an article *Chromolithography and Color Woodblock: Handmaidens to Nineteenth-Century Children's Literature* by John R. McNair, and the *Journal of Technical Writing and Communication ,Volume 21, Number 3* an article titled *Ancient Memory Arts and Modern Graphics* by John R. McNair, University of North Carolina, Charlotte, and in the journal *Neophilologus, Volume 68, Number 2*, a review of *An early "Hard word" list: Stephen Batman's "A note of saxon wordes'* . John also wrote an introduction to a facsimile reproduction of Stephen Batman's 1581 book, *"The doome warning all men to the judgement* "; and there are others, but these give an idea of the scope of John's wide-ranging talents.

He is currently penning a fascinating book covering the science and the remarkable tales of the four summers that he spent on Kodiak Island, Alaska working for the U.S. Fish and Wildlife Department. On the lighter side of his talents, John is a whistler, and from the earliest memories of my youth he was always whistling some joyful tune, or some melancholy ballad of days gone by.

Also, anyone who has known John will tell you that a most impressive feature of his character is the fact that more than just being a gentleman, John is truly a *gentle man*. Lastly, I have had the great fortune of having him act as editor on this book.

Doyle Brian McNair

On St. Patrick's Day, March 17th, 1940, in Harrison, Arkansas, a third son, **Doyle Brian McNair** was born to the couple. Doyle, if you remember from the Introduction to this book, was the son who provided the gift of a McNair genealogy book to our father, and unwittingly started years of research for me; his remarkable memory of the stories of the early years of his parents and brothers has added immeasurably to the effort. The St. Patrick's birth date could not be more appropriate, for Doyle was a fiery redhead, often with a fiery temper, well befitting his Scot-Irish ancestry. As father time has bleached some of the color from his hair, so has he cooled the temper, but Doyle still retains a razor sharp, and very wry wit, and a generosity born of a sensitive insight of others. As one recent example, after enjoying a meal at a favorite restaurant, Doyle left a "tip" consisting of a book on music, because the waitress had expressed her love of the subject to him on a previous visit. Certainly better than a 15% or 20% bit of coin, is a 100% bit of heart.

Early childhood was chaotic for Doyle and his brothers. First, a move from Arkansas to Wichita, Kansas, and then just two months past Doyle's fourth birthday, David was pulled into the army due to WWII, following which came Sibyl's illness, resulting in the four sons being placed into "The Children's Home" (a euphemism for an orphanage) where the younger boys were separated from their older brothers. Four is a little young to think that you have lost both of your parents, along with your older brothers, and now you are on your own, with a three year old brother in your charge. Fortunately, (or not fortunately to hear Doyle tell it) these two younger boys were spared more than just a brief stay in the children's home, and were temporarily placed with their dad's sister, Irene, and her husband John Strunk, both very stern disciplinarians. Over the next two years the chaos continued, with David's release from the army, his divorce and remarriage, (which was needed to regain custody of his children), and then another move, this time to Pueblo, Colorado. A succession of various homes there finally ended in some measure of stability, with the purchase of the home on O'Neal Ave., where the family remained for the next thirteen years. After graduation from Central High School in Pueblo, Doyle obtained an AA degree from Pueblo Junior College and then moved to Greeley, to attend Colorado State College, now known as The University of Northern Colorado. Then, as now, this is the School of Education, with studies designed for developing teachers. Doyle had thought he would enjoy teaching History, but after a quarter at Greeley he realized that would not suit him, so he moved again, to attend the University of Colorado in Boulder, pursuing studies in Political Science, History, and Literature.

Unfortunately, his studies were interrupted, for the War in Vietnam was raging, and Doyle was swept up by the draft in February of 1965. His Army Basic Training took place at Fort Leonard Wood, in Missouri, followed by AIT school in Fort Knox, Kentucky. Doyle had the good fortune however, to not have to serve in Vietnam, instead being assigned to the 840th Armored Division based at Fort Wainwright, on the outskirts of Fairbanks, Alaska. Discharged honorably in 1967, Doyle visited with me and my wife for a few weeks at our apartment in Rancho Cordova, California, where I was stationed at Mather Air Force Base at the time. He then returned to Boulder, Colorado, and found work at Fred's Columbine Cafe, learning the skills of a cook, a skill that he would pursue as a lifelong career. Doyle worked with Fred when he took over the restaurant of the Boulderado Hotel, and further honed his skills. In 1981 Doyle began cooking for the University of Colorado at Darly Commons, preparing breakfast and lunch for about 300 students daily. He continued there until his retirement in 2003. Doyle is an avid collector of coins, books, and sports memorabelia, and is one of those people you might hear about who can find unknown treasures at yard sales and the Goodwill store. Doyle never married, and still lives today in Boulder, Colorado.

Michael Price McNair

Michael Price McNair, the fourth son, was born close to Mother's Day, on May 7th, 1941, in Wichita, Kansas. He was the fourth and final son born to David and Sibyl, and was the first child born after the family had left their Ozark Mountain homeland, and the first to be born in a hospital, rather than at home. Like his brother Doyle, Michael was a red-head. Michael was the child who always had it easy in school, and while we brothers had to work hard for our grades, Michael would skim over his assignments, always pulling high marks without breaking a sweat. In his high school and junior college years Mike met a neighbor who was an electronic engineer, and by agreeing to play chess with him in exchange for lessons, Michael learned electronics from top to bottom. He was so well schooled in the field that when he began studies at the University of Colorado at Boulder, he soon realized that he knew the subject better than his professors, and quit the school after one or two terms. His early education in the emerging electronics industry would serve Michael very well for the rest of his life. After leaving school, Michael began his career with an electronics firm in Broomfield, a small town between Boulder and Denver.

In those early days of technology that would give rise to Silicon Valley, Michael worked at making printed circuits for the new transistor radios by drawing circuits on copper-on-fiberglass and etching them in a bathtub. In 1966 Michael had begun working at Fairchild Semiconductor in California, where he rubbed shoulders with some of the most influential men in the industry, including Robert Noyce and Gordon Moore who founded Intel in 1968, and with Andy Grove, who went on to become the CEO of Intel.

After Fairchild, Michael went on to work at Raytheon, and eventually Corso-Gray Industries, where he served as the International Sales Director, traveling to Europe, Japan, China, Singapore, Hong Kong, Russia, and more.

Michael was an inventor and Silicon Valley entrepreneur, and founded several businesses, including MikRo International in Singapore, which was acquired by a Japanese firm in 1997. After that, Michael initiated VeriTest, an electronics capital equipment firm, and Nanovega, a biotech firm in southern California. At the time of his death in 2011, Michael was the President of VeriTest, and the Chief Administration Officer of Nanovega.

The following is an excerpt from Michael's obituary:

Michael and his brother John had an opportunity to spend a summer on Kodiak Island, Alaska, working for US Fish and Wildlife, doing research on Kodiak bears and red salmon. It was an experience he cherished for many years as he regaled family and friends with stories about his encounters with huge bears and life on Kodiak Island.

It was also in Boulder, where he met Rose Marie, his wife. They had celebrated their 45th anniversary this year [2011]. Together they had enjoyed golfing, travel, gardening, cooking and entertaining their friends.

Michael's talents included his ability to draw and paint in many mediums, He also enjoyed wood carving, and just puttering around his garden in Soquel, where they resided surrounded by wonderful neighbors for 35 years. Michael is survived by his beloved family: his wife, Rose Marie and sons, Peter Trenton and Keith David and sons from a prior marriage, Sean and Adrian; his brothers John, Doyle and Roger, all his precious grandchildren, and many nieces and nephews. Preceding him in death were his mother Sibyl, father David and stepmother, Kathryn and his oldest brother, Norman. He will be fondly remembered by all who had the good fortune to know this wonderful man.

Before leaving Pueblo for the university in Boulder, Mike had met and married Donna Jean Tompkins, daughter of William E. Tompkins and Nola Maxine Hagar, both originally of Kansas. To the couple were born two sons, Sean Robert, in 1962, and Adrian William, in 1964. Both of these sons married and have children of their own. Michael and Donna divorced shortly before the birth of their second son but Donna remarried to Robert Bosley who helped raise the boys and was a good father and grandfather and Great-grandfather until his passing in March of 2015.

Sean David McNair married Marjorie (Marji) Louise Green and they had a daughter and a son. Their daughter is Jennifer (Jen) Kathline born in Pueblo, Colorado in 1981. Jen married Tim Leasure and in 2001 they had a son named Dylan. Jen is currently divorced. Sean and Marji's son is Sean Robert, born in 1987 in Pueblo, who is unmarried at this time.

Adrian William McNair (also known as Maverick) married Tracy Elaine (Buffy) Trehearne who was born in 1967 in Riverton, Wyoming. Buffy has worked for the U.S Postal Service and is currently a Certified Nurse's Aide. Three children were born to this couple: Miles Francis in 1988 at Casper, Wyoming; KayCee Lee in 1991 at La Junta, Colorado; and Kaitlin in 1996 at Logan, Utah. Adrian rode broncos on the rodeo circuit, possibly accounting for having every child born in a different state. Adrian and Buffy divorced in 2015 after thirty years of marriage. Two of their children have married and started families of their own. Miles, now a Baptist preacher, married Heather Lee Mann, and they have two daughters: Fae Lynn and Piper Elaine. KayCee Lee married Chase Edmonds, and they have one daughter, Bllayr Eve (the spelling Bllayr is unique but correct).

Michael Price McNair married a second time, to Rose Marie Klay who was born April 4, 1941 in Bon Carbo, Colorado, the Daughter of Peter Klay and Mary Bacich. Peter was born in

Colorado in 1910 and Mary was born in 1915 in Gospic, Croatia. Peter's parents, both born in Gospic, Croatia were Peter Henry Hlaj, (anglicized to Klay by the authorities on arrival at Ellis Island) and Ursula Lena Bregant. Petar Hlaj immigrated to America on the ship L'Aquitaine, sailing out of Le Havre, France on March 26, 1904, arriving in New York City on April 6th. His accommodation was in steerage, and he had $42.00 in his pocket. His listed destination was Salida, Colorado, to work in the coal mines.

Four years later, January of 1908, Ursula Lena Bregant arrived in New York aboard the La Loraine of Le Havre. Her final destination was listed as Primero, Colorado, which was a coal mining town built, starting in 1901, by the CF&I, (Colorado Fuel and Iron) that needed coal for the blast furnaces at its steel mill in Pueblo. At its peak, Primero's mines produced 3,000 tons of coal a week and employed an average of 600 men at a time, sixty percent of whom were foreign born.

Ursula was listed on the ship's manifest as coming from Fbure, Austria, and her mother's name, Maria, was listed as nearest relative, still living in Fbure. I have been unable to find a town or village by that name, even referencing maps of 1908 for Austria, Hungary, Bohemia, Croatia, or Slovenia. The name Fbure may have been just an area in Gospic or a neighborhood name. The company town of Primero, Colorado is long since a ghost town. Many coal miners gave their lives there, in multiple accidents, including explosions in 1907, and 1910, killing twenty-four, and seventy-four miners respectively. Ursula and Peter were married one year after her arrival, in January, 1909.

Peter, Ursula, Peter Jr. and Mary went back to the old country for a visit, and returned on the ship S.S. Paris, sailing out of Le Havre, France, on Nov. 8th, and arriving at the Port of New York on Nov. 15th, 1924. Pete showed his naturalization as having occurred in Trinidad, Colorado under passport number 473142. Ursula claimed naturalization by marriage, January 1909 in Trinidad. Young Peter is shown as age twelve, having been born in Feb. 1912 with sister Mary born in 1915, both in Trinidad. The info on the kids conflicts with the 1920 and 1930 census records which both indicate the kids to be two years older. Both census records also show Mary born in Kansas.

Mary Bacich's parents were Henry Bacich and Anna Yengich, and both of them were also born in Gospic, Croatia. Henry Bacich immigrated to the U.S. in 1922, leaving his wife and family behind in Gospic, Croatia. His contact in Colorado was his wife Anna Yengich's brother, Nick, who had immigrated in 1906 and was working in the Bon Carbo Coal Camp near Trinidad. Henry's wife and children immigrated to join him in 1929, per the 1930 U.S. census.

Michael Price McNair and Rose Marie had two sons also: Peter Trenton (Trent) in 1969 and Keith David in 1970. Both were born in San Jose, California.

Peter Trenton married twice, the first being with Dianne Keller, and they had one daughter in 1995, named Serena Dianne, who is in college now and working in journalism. Trent's second marriage is with Linda Elizabeth Garcia, the daughter of August (Augie) Garcia and Laura Alonso. Linda's parents emigrated from Cuba after the takeover of that country by Fidel Castro, and Linda was born in the U.S. Trent and Linda have a son named Aidan Garcia McNair who was born in 2003.

Keith David McNair is unmarried but does have a teenage son named Kyle, whose mother is Linda Williams.

Returning now to the subject of this chapter, **David Cleborn McNair**, who married second Kathryn Ada Rogers (see chapter eight) on September 24th, 1945 in Raton, New Mexico, en route to their new home in Colorado.

David was elevated to the position of General Agent for Farmers and Bankers Life Insurance and served as manager for two additional agents in Pueblo. His successes there caused him to be recruited by the Sackman Insurance Agency that brokered a greater variety of insurance products and allowed him to further his sales skills. Additional opportunities arose when he was asked to join Sears Roebuck and Company, where he acted briefly as a salesman before being elevated to the position of manager in the Installed Home Improvement (IHI) department and he spent several years in that position. The duties he assumed there were to arrange for installations of chain link fencing, roofing, storm doors and windows, kitchen remodels, and more. During the same timeframe, David's wife, Kathryn was also working as the secretary for the Pueblo Board of Realtors, so with the extra income and the experience gained at Sears, the couple started a new business named McNair Fence and Supply. Unfortunately, Pueblo's economy took a downturn at the same time. Workers at CF&I, the Colorado Fuel and Iron Company, a steel mill, went on an extended strike and the fledging fencing company folded just a year or so later. Fortunately, a new housing developer, Hoffman Homes, was beginning a new project called Beulah Heights on the West side of Pueblo and David managed to land the sales position for the project, selling more than a hundred homes over the succeeding years, including one of the first, a three bedroom home on O'Neal avenue to himself in 1953. When that development was finished another project called Lynn Gardens provided similar employment.

David and Kathryn had many friends in Pueblo and among them was a couple named Floyd and Wilma Marriot who operated a very successful second-hand store that carried thousands of comic books (my favorite when visiting) and many firearms (David's favorite). It was this friendship that in 1966 provided impetus for the family to once again take to the road and move to San Pablo, California where David and Kathryn bought two second-hand stores, consolidated the merchandise into one, and opened Mac's Trading Post on 23rd Street.

Soon David built racks along one wall to fill with hunting rifles, and display cases for handguns. Once the required Federal Firearms License was procured, Mac was in business. All too young, Mac passed away after a battle with cancer in 1970 at just age sixty-one. Kathryn was faced with the formidable task of learning enough about the firearms business to be able to continue it, and learn she did. "Mrs. Mac", as she soon became known to her customers, was successful to a great degree and ran the store until she sold it in 1979 at age seventy-one. I was treated to a story after her death, at age ninety-nine, in 2008, by the man who was the San Pablo Chief of Police. He told me that when he was a rookie in the police department that he learned more about guns from "Mrs. Mac" than from any other source.

Kathryn was a member of the National Rifle Association, and was such an active and well known member of the Richmond Rod and Gun Club that she wielded considerable authority. Once, on a visit, Kathryn wanted to take me down to the clubs firing range but when we arrived the overseer was just closing the gate for the day. Kathryn insisted that he was closing too early and when he resisted her entreaties, she got out of the car, waving her pistol, saying "Open the gate Buster!" The humor here is that 'Buster' was actually his name!

Now back to Colorado briefly for one more event, that being the birth of David's fifth son, and Kathryn's only, your author, Roger Bruce McNair in Pueblo on New Year's Day in 1947.

Roger Bruce McNair

Roger graduated from South High School in 1965 and in 1966 moved to California to help set up Mac's Trading Post. Later that year he joined the Air Force and was trained to work on auto-pilot and compass systems on B-52's and KC-135's and RC-135's (bombers, refueling tankers, and reconnaissance aircraft). He finished a four year tour with the rank of sergeant with postings at Mather Air Force Base in California, Barksdale Air Force Base in Louisiana and Eilison Air Force Base outside Fairbanks, Alaska, and after discharge began work as an Associate Engineer at Western Electric, the engineering arm of AT&T. He worked there until 1977 and then moved to Lebanon, Oregon where he worked for Sears in the same department, Installed Home Improvement, which his father had managed back in Pueblo.

In 1983 Roger changed again, into Allstate Insurance and owned an agency in Salem, Oregon until retiring in 2001. He then moved, in 2003, to California and cared for his mother until her death in 2008, just a few months shy of her 100th birthday.

In 1967, while stationed at Mather, Roger married Susan Mae Rippy, daughter of Luther and Virginia (Burden) Rippy, both originally of Oklahoma. Susan's paternal grandparents were Charles Barry Rippy of North Carolina and his wife Johnny May Anderson of Tennessee. Her maternal grandparents were John William Burden of Texas and Conzada Oda Womack of Oklahoma.

Roger and Susan had one son in 1968 named Shannon Patrick McNair, born in Richmond, California. Shannon served a tour in the Air Force and studied the Russian language at the Defense Language Institute in Monterey, California. After that training he was assigned to a post in Augsburg, Germany. I would tell you what his job was, but then I would have to kill you. After the service Shannon spent six months in Japan as an English language tutor, and there he met his future bride-to-be, Akiko Matsuu, a native of Honmachi, Yame, Fukuoka in that country. Akiko's parents were Tsuyoshi Matsuu and Hamako Nakashima. Her paternal grandparents were Masaji and Kane Matsuu, and her maternal grandparents were Satoru and Katsua Nakashima.

Akiko had a Bachelor's degree in English, had earned a teacher's certificate, and was employed as an English teacher. After passport and visa arrangements were made, Akiko moved to

Oregon and the couple was married in Salem in 1991. Shannon received a bachelor's degree in English from Willamette University in Salem and he and Akiko both attended Western Oregon University studying computer science. They were able to put that education to use before finishing, obtaining good employment in the field and Akiko did return to the school later and completed a B.S. degree in computer science. They currently live in Beaverton, Oregon, and have a daughter, Annika Matsuu McNair born in 2003, and a son, Aidan Matsuu McNair born in 2006. Both children were born in Beaverton.

The five sons of David Cleborn McNair from left to right:
Norman, Doyle, Michael, John, and Roger (1970)

The following two chapters will present the ancestral heritage for David Cleborn McNair's two wives, Sibyl Barnett and Kathryn Rogers.

Chapter 7   Sibyl Gertrude Barnett
First wife of David Cleborr. McNair

Sibyl Gertrude Barnett

Much of Sibyl's ancestry, the McNair, Allen, Price, Scherertz, and Manes lines, has been covered in the first four chapters of this book because her great-grandfather was James Claiborne McNair. But there are other lines to cover for her including, of course Barnett, and also Pruitt, Green, Grinder, Reeves, and Brown. In addition, we will learn of a family blood feud that garnered national news coverage, and of a connection to the death of Meriwether Lewis, of Lewis and Clark fame.

I will start with Sibyl's father, David Jackson Barnett, and then come back to her mother, Gertrude Pruitt, and follow both lines back to their time of service in the Revolutionary War.

David Jackson Barnett was born in Gilbert, Searcy County, Arkansas on October 6th, 1888. On May 1st, 1910, he married Gertrude Pruitt, and they had six children. Sibyl was the first born, on July 9th, 1911, followed by Joe Clinton in 1913, Alfred (Alf) Jackson in 1916, David (DJ) Jackson in 1918, Katherine Bernelle in 1922, who died young in 1924, and David Kenneth in 1925. With the exception of Katherine who died at age two, all of the remaining children spent their adult lives in the Sacramento, Placerville, Rocklin area of California, working on the railroad in that area.

At the 1910 Federal census, David Jackson Barnett was listed as a farmhand on his father's farm, but by the 1920 census he was listed as a teacher at the Bruno High School. David died when Sibyl was just thirteen years old. His obituary appeared in:

THE MARSHALL REPUBLICAN, Searcy County Oct. 17
1924.
David Jackson Barnett
A sadness born of a genuine love and appreciation of his worth and manhood rests over this community for many a day as the result of the untimely death of David Jackson Barnett, which occurred Tuesday, Oct. 7. The deceased was born Oct. 6, 1888, his birthplace being near the present boundary line between Saint Joe and Tomahawk Townships. He was the son of Mr. and Mrs. J. H. Barnett, and present resident of Marshall. He was educated in the schools of this county and in the high school at Western Grove. For almost twenty years he was one of Searcy County's most successful teachers, and the love he engendered in the hearts of the children and the benefits of character and intellect he gave them will be his enduring monument. Last spring he was appointed postmaster at Gilbert, and in this as in

everything that he did, his work was characterized by proficiency and courteous consideration for those he served.

He leaves a wife, who before her marriage to him was Gertrude Pruitt, and five children: Sibyl, Joe, Alf, D.J., and Burnell. The oldest child is 13 and the youngest 2. His parents and several brothers and sisters also survive him.

His funeral services were from the home of his sister, Mrs. H. K. Ramsay, Wednesday, and interment was in the Osborn cemetery. Perhaps the largest crowd ever assembled at a burial there gathered to pay him their tribute of love and respect. His services were in charge of the members of the Masonic lodge, in which order he had held high honors. F. G. Hollabaugh made a few remarks by way of introduction and paid a high tribute to the character and accomplishments of the departed brother. S. E. Hollabaugh then completed the Masonic service and delivered one of the most beautiful and comforting addresses to which it has ever been our privilege to listen. Rev. John Battenfield spoke briefly with characteristic eloquence.

Words are all insufficient at such times as this either to express appreciation or to assuage grief. There can be no higher tribute to the life and character of David Jackson Barnett than the deep and abiding grief in the hearts of all who knew him. The only refuge from grief like this is in Him who has promised peace to those who come sorrowing.

And, from the Masonic Lodge, the following resolution:

Resolutions of Respect

To the Worshipful Master, Wardens and Brethren of St. Joe Lodge No. 317, F. and A. M: We, your Committee on Resolutions of Respect to the memory of Bro. D. J. Barnett, respectfully submit the following:

Whereas, That through the divine wisdom of the Allwise Creator, our esteemed brother D. J. Barnett, has been removed from our fraternal ranks, and who departed this life on the 7th day of October, 1924, at the age of 36 years; and

Whereas, That while we humbly submit to the will of the Great Creator, we feel keenly the loss to the fraternity and the community of a model and upright man, a dutiful husband and a Mason cut down in his prime; and

Whereas, Bro. Barnett was initiated into the mysteries of the fraternity on the 27th day of October, 1917, at the age of 29 years; was passed to the Degree of Fellowcraft November 24, 1917 and raised to the sublime degree of Master Mason December 22 of the same year, and took the higher degrees of Masonry at Marshall Chapter No. 96, R. A. M. He leaves a wife and four small children, to which we extend heartfelt sympathy; and

Whereas, Bro. Barnett had taught school most of the time since his early manhood and was considered one among the best educated of our community. He was postmaster at Gilbert at the time of his death. Bro. Dave, as he was commonly called was laid to rest in the Osborne cemetery the 18th day of October, 1924, with Masonic honors; now therefore be it Resolved, By St. Joe Lodge No. 317, F. and A. M. that a page be set apart in the lodge record for this resolution, a copy be furnished the Mountain Wave and the Marshall Republican, with the request that it be published, and a copy of each be furnished to the family of the deceased.

Fraternally submitted, S. M. ALLEN

David's father was John Henry Barnett born March 28th, 1869, in Tomahawk Township, Searcy County, Arkansas, as one of nine children of David Jackson Barnett and "Flurry" Grinder. Later I will trace the Grinder Family and their connection to the death of Meriwether Lewis. John Henry was the sheriff of Marshall, Arkansas, the county seat of Searcy County, and he was assassinated on June 9th, 1934. This brings us to the story of the Barnett-Henley feud.

The Barnett-Henley Feud

In Arkansas, trouble was brewing, for just a few months after the birth of David and Sibyl's first child, Norman, an ancient feud between the Barnett's and the Henley's erupted into life with the murder by ambush of Sibyl's uncle James "Vance" Barnett. No concrete evidence could link the murder to a member of the Henley clan, but it was widely speculated within the community. Sibyl's grandfather, and father of the murdered Vance, was the Sheriff of Marshall, the seat of Searcy County. His name was John Henry Barnett and he was hell-bent to prove the case, but never could to the satisfaction of the prosecuting attorney. The Henley's, on the other hand, were hell-bent to see John Henry dead. Late that year, Leland Henley lay in wait for John Henry, and when the Sheriff exited the barbershop on Main Street, Henley opened fire, but instead of killing the Sheriff, his shot hit and killed W. W. Findley, a popular merchant, who was walking alongside Barnett. Leland Henley was arrested, tried, convicted, and sent away on a life sentence. For reasons that I have not been able to determine, Henley returned to Marshall on a ten day furlough about one year later, in early December, 1933. On Christmas eve, shots were fired at Rupert Barnett, another of Sibyl's uncles, from the Henley family's restaurant, and John Henry along with his son, Oscar, responded to the scene, where the Sheriff and his two sons fired repeatedly on the restaurant, and fire was returned from inside. No one was killed, but John Henry was shot in the face, fortunately not a severe wound. He was hospitalized briefly in Little Rock. Threats of retaliation were flying from both camps, and the situation became so severe that Arkansas Governor Futtrell called out National Guard troops to quell the violence, which they did. Nevertheless, six months later, on June 9th, 1934, Sheriff John Henry Barnett was murdered. His assassin has never been identified. The troubles in Searcy County captured national attention. I found the following article in a New York newspaper:

From the Binghamton Press newspaper, Binghamton, NY 1933:
TROOPS CALLED
AS ANCIENT FEUD
FLARES ANEW
Arkansas Marshal Wounded as
He and Sons Bombard Cafe
Marshall, Ark., December 26— (Associated Press)
Quiet settled over this little community in the north Arkansas mountains today as National guard and county officers endeavored to establish peace between two families following revival of an ancient feud which has claimed two lives in recent years. City Marshal J. H. Barnett, 60, wounded slightly in Sunday's outbreak, was in a Little Rock hospital and expected to return during the day with his two sons to face service on a warrant he was notified had been Issued. The sons, Oscar and Rupert were arrested last night. The sudden battle that marred the Christmas observance here followed the reported return on furlough of Leland Henley, 29, sentenced to prison for life about a year ago for the slaying of W.W.   Findley, merchant, who was shot down while walking along the street with City Marshal Barnett by bullets generally believed intended for Barnett.
The city marshal and his two sons Sunday bombarded a restaurant operated by Henley's cousin, Alf, scene of another slaying less than two weeks ago. Leland's two brothers, Nobe and Jack, and his sister, Mrs. Bennie Mathews, were reported to have been in the restaurant from which numerous shots were fired back at the Barnett's. From his hospital bed the city marshal said the battle occurred when he went to the cafe after someone from inside had fired at Rupert as he walked past the building. The city marshal's sons said their brother had been slain in Searcy County from ambush, but the slayer or slayers never had been identified. Isaac Ragland, a farmer, was wounded fatally here only a few days ago as he sat in Henley's restaurant. The assassin [of Marshal Barnett] was never identified.

On October 2nd, 1887, John Henry Barnett married Tennessee Catherine Reeves. He was eighteen and she was sixteen years of age. Tennessee gave birth to their first child at age seventeen, and to their tenth at age forty-three. The children were: David Jackson, 1888; Martha Angeline, 1891; Ida Belle, 1894; Fitzhue Lee, 1898; Emily, 1900; James Vance, 1903 (killed in the feud); Oscar Scott, 1904; Rupert William, 1909; Opal Grace, 1912; and Edna Lavada in 1914. An interesting tidbit is the name Fitzhue Lee in 1898. He was apparently named after the man who was the U.S. Consul at the American Embassy in Havana, Cuba. That Fitzhue Lee was a nephew of General Robert E. Lee, and had recommended to President McKinley in 1898 against sending the U.S.S. Maine to the Havana Harbor. The mysterious explosion and sinking of that ship in the harbor led, in part, to the beginning of the Spanish-American War.

We know that John Henry Barnett was the Sheriff of Marshall, so it is interesting that his choice of a bride was named Reeves. In the past, in England, the equivalent of our term county was shire, and the chief law enforcement officer for the shire was called the reeve. From the term "shire reeve" comes the term "sheriff." Tennessee Catherine Reeves was born March 29th, 1871, in Tomahawk, Arkansas, the daughter of Fletcher Reeves and Emily Brown, a woman of German descent. Tennessee may have been given that name to honor the birthplace of her grandfather Peter Reeves, who was born in that state, as was his wife, Catherine Grinder. Catherine was the sister of "Flurry" Grinder, the wife of David Jackson Barnett, so John Henry Barnett and Tennessee Reeves were second cousins as well as husband and wife.

John Henry Barnett's father was David Jackson Barnett, born November 30th, 1827 in McMinn County, Tennessee. The following lines are excerpted from a letter as told to W. F. (Frank) Reeves in 1903 by Joshua Reeves and re-told to James Barnett by Frank Reeves, June 4, 1954:

In the autumn of 1845 David Barnett, age 18, came to Arkansas with a group by ox wagon train, leaving his home in McMinn County, Tennessee. The emigrants were seeking a home in the new state of Arkansas. They traveled over a military road from Memphis, Tennessee to Buffalo City, Arkansas then followed a country trail leading northwest until they came to a little place called Yellville. From there they went southwest to the Buffalo River, stopping in the Buffalo-Tomahawk section in December 1845 near Gilbert, Searcy Co., Arkansas. This was the only place the Buffalo was crossable at that time of the year. There were several other unmarried young people including Margaret Flora Grinder and her brother, Bob Grinder. All stayed and camped for the winter. David fell in love with one of the crew, Flurry Grinder, and they got married. They settled on the tract of land where they camped. They built a house and homesteaded the land and lived most of their lives at this place. Margaret Flurry Barnett, David's first wife, passed away October 12, 1878 [after having mothered his first ten children, including John Henry] and her grave stone in Osborn Cemetery near St. Joe carries the message that "She was a tender mother, a faithful friend, and a follower of Christ." David Barnett's second marriage was to Sarah Jane Cross on July 4, 1879. To this union was born one child, Noah Barnett on April 10, 1880. This marriage soon ended in divorce and Noah was raised by his mother at Tomahawk. David Barnett was married the third time on August 16, 1881 to Cynthia Reeves. To this marriage was born eight children but only two lived to be grown and raised families, namely Granville Murphy "Murph", and Absalum Andrew "Drew."

David Barnett served the Union during the Civil War, joining Company M, Arkansas 3rd Cavalry in February of 1864, and was discharged honorably after the war. He died in 1915.

John Henry Barnett 1869-1934

An extra story here that involves the Grinder Family:

Grinder's Stand

The Natchez Trace was a 550 mile trail from Natchez on the Mississippi river to Nashville through the wilderness of the Tennessee valley, in use by explorers, hunters, and Indians since 1733. On the Trace was Grinder's Stand, where weary travelers might find shelter and a meal. Owned by Robert and Priscilla Grinder, early settlers out of North Carolina, the Stand was composed of two small roughhewn cabins and a barn to shelter the animals. In the autumn of 1809, three men stopped and asked for lodging. Priscilla was wary because Robert was away working their farmland at Duck River, ten miles north, and not due back till morning. She and some of her younger children were alone and the Trace was notorious for pirates, thieves and murderers, but the demeanor and lawyerly speech of the visitors let her decide to accept the men. One was John Pernier, servant of the leader, one was a black man who was the slave of John Neeley, the government agent to the Chickasaw Indians, and the leader of the group was Meriwether Lewis. Lewis was on his way to Washington, D.C. to report to Thomas Jefferson on his exploration of the Western lands stretching to the Pacific Coast at the mouth of the Columbia River.

Jefferson had rewarded Lewis with the Governorship of the Louisiana Territory, but Lewis had found himself unable to reduce his findings to writing, and was greatly depressed by that, which had finally prompted this journey. Mrs. Grinder housed the other two men and the pack animals in the barn, and the children took food to them. She allowed Lewis the use of the second cabin, and prepared a meal for him. As darkness fell, Lewis spread a bearskin on the rude puncheon (wood) floor, wrapped himself in a buffalo robe, and retired for the night. It was Oct. 10th, and no one except perhaps the thirty-five year old Meriwether Lewis knew that this would be the last night of his life. Sometime during the night or early morning hours, Lewis put a pistol to his chest and another to his head, and fired them both. He is buried about 400 feet from Grinders Stand, and many years later a marker was erected there.

The accuracy of this cause of death is disputed by some historians and promoted by others. The other possibility is that of murder, but not at the hands of the Grinder family. Not long after this incident, Robert and Priscilla moved to Wayne County to be near Robert's brother John

Grinder. John Grinder's daughter, Margaret Flora (Flurry) Grinder was born in 1830, and in 1845, she joined an ox-wagon train bound for Arkansas. Also on that trip was her soon-to-be husband, David Jackson Barnett. Their son, John Henry Barnett, born March 29th, 1869 was the grandfather of Sibyl Gertrude Barnett.

Now back to the Barnett family. The parents of David Jackson were James Elemuel Barnett and Martha Kempt. James was born October 22, 1792 in Greenville, South Carolina, and Martha July 3rd, 1795 in Moore, North Carolina. David was the fifth of five children born to Martha, and she died when he was just eight. James married next Sarah Jane Arnold, thirty-three years James's junior, and she bore him three more children. James Elemuel was a Baptist preacher, and some historians say he fought in the War of 1812 under Colonel Andrew Jackson, though I was unable to verify that service. James died in 1869, at age seventy-two as a result of injuries he received from a fall. He died in the evening and Sarah died of grief the following morning. They were buried together in a single homemade casket, crafted of black walnut, in the Christian cemetery located between Latham and California, Missouri. During his time on earth, James had moved from South Carolina to Tennessee, then to Searcy County, Arkansas. During the Civil War, he and Sarah went first to Springfield, Missouri, then Tipton in that state, then to the farm near Latham where they resided until their death.

The father of James Elemuel was David Barnett born in Lunenburg, Virginia, July 31, 1755. His mother was Sarah Agnes Phillips, born circa 1755, in Greenville, South Carolina. James was the youngest of seven children; four sons and two daughters preceded him. They made their home in Greenville, South Carolina until her death in 1836, and his in 1839. The following is a partial transcription of his pension request for service in the militia during the Revolutionary War:

Pension application of David Barnett S17826 fn35NC
Transcribed by Will Graves
State of South Carolina, Greenville District
On this 10th day of October in the year of our Lord 1832 personally appeared in open court before the Judge of the Court of Common Pleas now sitting David Barnett a Resident of Greenville District and State of South Carolina aged 77 years who being first duly sworn according to law doth on his oath make the following

declaration in order to obtain the benefit of the act of Congress passed the seventh day of June 1832 that he entered the Service of the United States in the Year 1779 under the following named Officers and served as herein Stated, under Captain Berry Turner in the militia as a substitute in the place of David Warmuck for six months under Colonel William Moore, and marched from Caswell County in the State of North Carolina where he then resided to the battle of Stono in South Carolina and was in that battle, Served out the term and returned home, we being discharged by Captain Turner which he has lost. And in the year 1780 he again entered the Service of the US under Captain George Samuel in Caswell County North Carolina and served under General Gates, Colonel & Major not recollected, marched to Camden South Carolina and was in the battle when Gates was defeated, after which he rallied at Hillsboro North Carolina. Served out the six months the term for which he entered the Service the last time and was discharged in the Waxhaw Settlement. That in the year 1781 he volunteered for six months in the State of North Carolina and joined a company of mounted infantry and joined General Green and on meeting with an offer hired John Hudgins as a Substitute who served out the tour and brought him a discharge which is lost; That after the militia were classed and every four allowed to hire one Soldier for 18 months which should serve as a six months tour for that he and three others hired a Substitute for the 18 months, and paid him and got a discharge for a six months tour, the Substitute was named John Henry Prior. Then in 1782 he was drafted for three months under Captain Hargis who commanded at Hillsborough and served the tour out at that place as a guard for the public store, and that he volunteered in 1782 under Captain Arch. Deacon for the term of three months for the purpose of guarding the crossing place at Dan River, but does not recollect how much of the term he served.

And I hereby Relinquish every Claim whatever to a pension or an annuity except the present and I declare that my name is not on the pension Roll of any Agency of the State of South Carolina. Sworn and Subscribed the day and Year aforesaid.

Signed, David Barnett

Now we turn back to the mother of Sibyl Barnett, Gertrude Pruitt. I have not been able to identify a date for this photo, but they were married in 1910, and I would think the photo is in the 1910 to 1915 range. And by the way --- nice hat!

D.J. Barnett and Gertrude Pruitt

Gertrude's Parents were Solomon Clinton Pruitt and Harriet Susan McNair. This next photo is Solomon, who went by his middle name, Clinton, in circa 1906.

Other than the photo, I have little further information on Clinton. Sibyl Barnett had given the photo to my brother John, and on the back she had written that Clinton was speaking with an unidentified man regarding possible mineral deposits on Clinton's land.

95

There was a lead and zinc mining boom occurring in Searcy County, Arkansas in the 1906 timeframe. I have been unable to determine whether or not the Pruitt family was able to benefit from that activity. Clinton was born in February of 1852 in Cumberland County, Kentucky, and was one of eight children born to Granville Pruitt and Alison "Ailsey" Green. Granville and Alison were both born in Cumberland County, in 1827 and 1830 respectively. Nothing is known of Alison's family, and of Granville, only his father's name is known, and that was Solomon Pruitt Jr., (or Prewitt) born in North Carolina in 1801, but who spent most of his life in Cumberland County, Kentucky. Solomon Junior's mother is also unknown, but his father was Solomon Prewitt Sr.

Clinton Pruitt, left, discussing possible lead and zinc deposits on his land
Circa 1906

Solomon Prewitt Sr. was a Private during the Revolutionary War and he received a pension for his service. He was born in 1742 in Virginia and he entered the service of his country in 1777 at the age of thirty-six. He served with Captain John Nelson and Colonel Josiah Parker in the 2nd Regiment of the Virginia line until 1783. During his military career he participated in the battle of Brandywine at Chadds Ford, Pennsylvania, in 1777, Kings Mountain, North Carolina, in 1780, and the ultimate battle --- the surrender of the British Army by General Cornwallis at Yorktown, Virginia in October, 1781.*

Although Cornwallis' surrender spelled the de facto end of the war, it would be two years later, in 1783, before the Treaty of Paris was formally signed by Great Britain and the United States. Solomon served until that time and he was honorably discharged.

He brought his family to Cumberland County, Kentucky in late 1804 after he had lived for a period of time in North Carolina. He settled in the Bow community while his brother and other family members moved to Pea Ridge. The identity of his first wife is not known and because of his incredibly long life span there may have been other marriages that cannot be documented. It is known that he was married to Mary Dulwitt in either late 1840 or early 1841. He was about ninety-eight years old at the time; and he lived until 1852 when he died at the age of 110. His wife, Mary, subsequently applied for and received a Revolutionary War widow's pension in 1853. She was eighty-seven years old at the time.

The above military information is from Revolutionary War pension records located in the national archives.

On Aug. 20, 1852, the Will of SOLOMON PREWITT was recorded. The Will had been written Feb. 1, 1844 (Cumberland, Kentucky Bk E.)

The last will and testament of Solomon Prewitt of the County of Cumberland, Kentucky State. I, Solomon Prewitt, considering the uncertainty of the mortal life and being of sound mind and memory, do make and publish this my last will and testament in manner and form following this is to say, I give and bequeath unto my beloved wife Merry Prewitt all my estate, save my heirs one cent apiece, and I, Solomon Prewitt hereby give all my land and the claims and (illegible) thereunto, to Mary Prewitt, my wife, at my decease. This the first day of February, in the year of our Lord one thousand eight hundred and forty four.
Solomon (his ^{X}mark) Prewitt.
Signed, sealed, published and declared by the above named Solomon Prewitt to be his last will and testament in the presence of us, who at his request and in his presence have inscribed our names as witnesses thereto.

John Dulwit.
Charles Smith

Solomon's will is a tribute to brevity and succinctness, and also to optimism, as he apparently waited until he was 102 years of age to produce it, and left everything to his *young* bride. But, since he had lived so long, he probably had many, many, other possible heirs --- children, grandchildren, great-grandchildren, and likely great-great-grandchildren. Had they all come to the proceedings to claim their share, at one cent apiece, it could have cost Mrs. Prewitt a buck or two! Atta boy, Solomon! Well done!

Chapter 8   Kathryn Ada Rogers
Second wife of David Cleborn McNair

A number of years ago, my mother told me that she had given herself the middle name of Ada. She claimed that she had not been given a middle name at birth because her mother, Carrie Charlotte Burton, wanted her to have, for a middle name, the number "Eight", but her father, Rodney Fridley Rogers, would not agree to it. Consequently, she says she choose Ada so that her initials would be KAR, which was the spelling used by a luxury auto called the Kissell Kar. I surmise that there is a big grain of truth to Kathryn's story, for what she did not know when she told me that story was that the name of her great-great-grandmother was Catherine *Eights*. In turn, the great-grandfather of Catherine Eights was Willem Echt. The records of the Dutch Reformed Church in New York (previously New Amsterdam) record the marriage banns of Willem Echt, from Rotterdam, Netherlands, and Marritje (Maria) Van Dyke from Amsterdam, on December 10, 1699. I have only been able to confirm one child for this couple, although there likely would have been more.

The one I can confirm was Abraham Eights, born in March of 1710. In time, Abraham married Catherine Benson and raised a family of three daughters and two sons, named Elizabeth, Maria, Abraham, Willem, and Catherina. The third child, Abraham, was born on May 15, 1745, and in time moved north to Albany, NY, where he married Catherine Brooks, and raised a family of ten children. It was the third child of this couple, Catherine, born Jan. 11, 1776 for whom Carrie Charlotte Burton wished to bestow upon Kathryn the middle name of Eights.

Abraham Eights moved to Albany in 1766 and built himself a home on the waterfront at 28 Dock Street, and began his trade as a sail maker, eventually becoming the most respected and sought after sail maker in the area. Four years after his arrival, in June of 1770, he married Catherine Brooks in St. Peter's Anglican Church. In 1790, the Eights family changed their religious affiliation and became members of the Presbyterian Church on South Pearl street, where Abraham served as an elder for the last thirty years of his life, until his death on Jan. 10, 1820. In addition to his sail making, he served as a fireman, as a Lieutenant in the Albany Militia in 1775-76, and as the city's Dockmaster. It must have been somewhat disconcerting, as a sail maker, when Robert Fulton steamed into the Albany Docks in 1807, in his steamboat, the Clermont.

Of the ten children born to Abraham and Catherine, only two were sons, Abraham and Jonathan, and of those two, only Jonathan survived to adulthood. Though he was raised on the waterfront, Jonathan chose to pursue a different path, becoming a physician with a private practice, but also serving Albany's poor as the Almshouse physician. He married Alida Wynkoop, and they had three children, of which one was James Eights, who became a man of science and art. He was a draftsman on the geological survey for the Erie Canal, one of the founders of the Albany Lyceum of Natural History, and in 1827, he became an examiner at an Engineering College established in Troy, NY, by his friend, Stephen Van Rensselaer. That school evolved into what is today known as Rensselaer Polytechnic Institute.

In 1829, James, serving as a naturalist, sailed on a scientific expedition to Antarctica, and published biological and geological accounts of his findings there. James was a talented watercolorist as well, and beginning in the 1840's he painted from the memories of his youth and historical research, street scenes as Albany had appeared in the early years of the 19th century. One of those paintings was of St. Peter's Anglican Church where his grandfather had married in 1770.

St. Peter's Anglican Church, corner of State and Chapel.
Watercolor by James Eights

101

Moving back a step now, to the third child, daughter Catherine, born to the sail maker, Abraham, and his wife, Catherine Brooks. Catherine Eights married John Burton on Jun. 2, 1795 in the First Presbyterian Church of Albany. John Burton was born Sep. 14, 1764 into a family that had already been living in the American Colonies for more than 130 years. The progenitor of the Burtons in America was Boniface Burton, who had been born in England in 1556, and died in Lynn, Massachusetts in June of 1669, at the age of 113. He was listed as a resident of Lynn as early as 1630, and as a freeman there in 1635. The only name found for his wife is her given name of Frances, and the great likelihood is that she was also from England.

The son of Boniface was John Burton, who is found as a freeman in neighboring Salem, Mass. in 1638. It is not known whether John was born in England or in the Massachusetts colony, but we do know that his occupation was as a tanner of leather, and that was a critical part of the process in making shoes, for which Lynn, Mass. was held in such high regard as to then be considered the shoe making capital of the world. The artful use of taxes and tariffs, making other shoe manufacturers goods more expensive, of course, probably played as much a role as did the quality of the Lynn shoes.

John Burton's wife was Frances Thornton, and from there the line of descent then runs through their son Isaac, with wife Hannah, and then Isaac's son, Jacob, with wife Mary Lidah Herrick, on to son Josiah Burton and wife Susannah Winans, and finally to their son John, being the Burton who married Catherine Eights.

This union produced 5 sons, Stephen A., Abraham Eights, William E., James, and Charles Edward, along with 4 daughters, Susannah B., Catherine, Mary, and Amelia.
I will come back to the union and children of Burton and Eights shortly, but first a little on the family of Mary Lidah Herrick, being the family that I have traced back further in time than any other in this book.

I suppose every family wishes for a little royalty in the family tree, so here is mine. I begin in Sweden, with Sigurd (Ring) Randversson, who was born in AD 730, who took Alfhild Gandolfsdottir (daughter of Gandolf), of Denmark, as his wife. A child of theirs was Ragnar (Lodbrok) Sigurdsson, born in 760, in Uppsala, Sweden, who married a cousin, Aslaug

Sigurdsdottir, who was born in 765, in Denmark. That couple's son was Sigurd (Snake Eye) Ragnarsson, born in Denmark in 786. He married a woman named Heluna Bleja, who was born in England to a Viking invader and an English Woman, in 784. The son born to this couple, in Denmark, in 814, was Harthacnute (Knud) Sigurdsson. Knud's wife is unknown, but she was the mother of a king, Geva (Gorm the Old) Knudsson, born in Denmark, becoming the King of Denmark in about 900, and ruling until his death in 958.

Gorm the Old is the first historically recognized King of Denmark, although his father, Knud, had deposed the prior "ruler" of Denmark, and ruled the land until his death, when Gorm was named King. Although some reports say that Gorm ruled all of Denmark, it is more likely that he ruled only that portion called Jutland. King Gorm was married to Thyra Dannebod, and they had three sons, namely, Toke, Knut, and Harald.

Harald went on to become King of Denmark, and for the last fifteen years of his life was also King of Norway. He was known as King Harald (Bluetooth) Gormsson. The nickname Bluetooth supposedly was given due to Harald's love of Blueberries, which stained his teeth. Today, Bluetooth wireless communication devices are named after him, and the logo for Bluetooth is made from the runes of the letters H and B.

The child born to Bluetooth and his concubine, Gunnhild, about 975, and it is with this child that we finally are close to the eventual name of Herrick for the family tree. The child's name was Ericke Haraldsson. His brother, Sweyn (Forkbeard) Haraldsson went on to claim the throne, so Ericke was back to semi-commoner status, and thus the genealogical trail is much reduced, and the names of wives are lost to time for a few generations, but the trail does lead on. A son born to Ericke and his wife was Eric the Forester, born in Denmark about 1060, who went raiding into England, and ended up staying there. He was a ruler of East Anglia of that country, and raised a fighting force against William the Conqueror when he invaded from Normandy. Eric the Forester failed in battle, and was required to become a commander of a portion of William's army. His subsequent loyalty to William allowed him to obtain land in Leicestershire, England, and he retired to his home there when he was old.

The next four generations of this family all went by the name Henry Eyryk, born respectively in about 1125, 1175, 1216, and 1250. These were followed by John in 1275, Robert, about 1300, William Eyrick, about 1320, another William, about 1355, and one more William, born about 1424. Next is Robert in 1450, whose wife was Agnes, and whose son was Thomas, born in 1479. The son born to Thomas was John, born in about 1513. All of these men and their families continued in the Leicestershire area.

The tombstone of John Heyrick and his wife, Mary Bond, is in St. Martin's church, Leicester, at the east end of the north aisle, in a part once called "Heyrick's Chancel." His epitaph reads:

> Here lieth the body of John Heyrick, late of this Parish, who departed this life 2d of Aprill, 1589, being about the age of 76. He did marry Marie, daughter of John Bond of Wardende, in the Countie of Warwicke, Esquire, and did live with the said Mary, in one house, full fifty-two yeares; and in all that tyme, never buried man, woman, or child, though they were sometimes twenty in household. He had yssue by said Marie, 5 sonnes and seven daughters. The said John was Mayor of this town in anno 1559, and again in anno 1572. The said Marie departed this life ye 8th day of December, 1611, being of the age of 97 years. She did see before her departure, of her children, and her children's children, and their children, to the number of 142.

In 1557, to John Heyrick and Marie Bond, a son was born, and named William. When knighted in 1605, he became Sir William Heyrick.

> Sir William Herrick was born in Leicester, removed to London in 1574 to reside with his brother Nicholas, then an eminent banker in Cheapside. He attached himself to the court and was known as a man of great abilities and remarkably handsome. He was high in the confidence of Queen Elizabeth, as well as of King James, and by honorable service to both, acquired large properties. He was a Member of Parliament between 1601 and 1630, knighted in 1605. Beau Manor Park was purchased by Sir William and has been in the possession of his descendants for over 275 years. It is the "headquarters" for the Herrick race. William's picture at Beau Manor exhibits him with a picked beard, a large ruff, and in a white satin doublet, which he used on Christmas day, attending Queen Elizabeth. He wears a sword and over his dress hangs loosely a large black cloak. In one hand are his gloves, the other, elevated to his breast, holds the stump and tassels of his ruff. Under the photo is His motto 'Sola supereminet virtus'. (Wikipedia)

Sola supereminet virtus' means virtue alone is paramount.

Sir William Heyrick's trade was that of goldsmith and lapidary, and he was the Royal Jeweler to King James I. In the *Diary of the Rev. Henry Newcome (Sept.30, 1661 to Sept. 29, 1663)*, it is reported that the act which caused King James to bestow knighthood upon him was that William skillfully drilled a hole through the diamond that King James then wore. Burial is at the Cathedral Church of St Martin, Leicester, Leicestershire, England. The grave is at the north wall of the choir inside the Church. Sir William and Lady Joan (nee May) Herrick had a dozen children, and the fifth was a son named Henry, born in Leicester, August 16th, 1604.

Henry is the original immigrant for the Herrick line, arriving in the Massachusetts Bay Colony in 1630, settling in Salem, and later moving to Beverly. He died there after November 24, 1670, when his will was drawn, and before March 15, 1671, when the inventory of his estate was done. Henry married Editha Laskin, the daughter of Hugh Laskin of Salem. To this union were born nine sons and a daughter. The line of descent is through Ephraim Herrick, born February 11th, 1637. One of Ephraim's brothers, Henry Herrick Jr., served on the jury trying Rebecca (Towne) Nurse in 1692, during the Salem Witch Trials. She was found guilty and was executed.

Ephraim Herrick wed Mary Cross and they were the parents of five sons and three daughters. The fourth child was Stephen, who wed Elizabeth Trask. This union produced ten children, the eighth of which was a daughter named Mary Lidah Herrick, who became the wife of Jacob Burton. That is the Herrick line, from Viking warriors, to Danish Kings, back to warriors and commoners; a member of the British Parliament; a knighthood bestowed by King James I; to Pilgrim immigrants; a worthy, but heady, line of folks. Now, we turn our attention back to the family of Burton, with whom Kathryn Ada (Rogers) McNair's mother shares her maiden name.

The firstborn of John Burton and Catherine Eights, Stephen A. Burton, was born on Aug. 9, 1813, in Schenectady, New York, and became a farmer like his father, but he also had the wanderlust in him, and moved first to Blandford, Massachusetts, where he met and married Charlotte Jackson on Feb. 4, 1835. They had eight children there, but then moved their family to Grafton, Illinois by 1860. Charlotte died in 1868, and by 1870 Stephen Burton had moved again, to Campbell, Missouri with his youngest three children, ages 15 to 20, still in tow. By 1880, he had moved again, to Madison, Nebraska, where he was living with his son, Charles Justice and his wife. Stephen died on Christmas Eve, 1889, in Lincoln, Nebraska. The names of his children were

Catherine Amelia, Mary Elizabeth, Margaret Jane, James Ezra, Lucia Delinda, Charles Justice, Charlotte Melissa, and Edward Augustus.

The last born child for Stephen and Charlotte was Edward Augustus Burton, born Aug. 28, 1855 in Blandford, Massachusetts. Edward was also destined for life as a farmer, but though his father left Missouri north to Nebraska, Edward headed south, and is found in the 1880 census in Prairie Township, Washington County, Arkansas. There, on Jan. 1, 1879, he married Mary Belle Peer.

The original Peer immigrant to the American Colonies was Jan Teunissen Pier, who was born in Amsterdam, Holland, and came to New Amsterdam (now New York City) sometime before the birth of his son Teunis Jansen Pier in 1664. The name eventually anglicized to Peer as the son moved on to New Jersey, where the family stayed for 5 generations, but as the Peers were loyalists to the British Crown, the family moved to Ontario, Canada during the American Revolution. Two generations later, Jacob Peer, born in Ontario, had repatriated to the U.S., and is found on the 1830 Census in North East Township, Erie County, Pennsylvania, and later in La Porte, Indiana. It is Jacob's son Edward, born in Pennsylvania in 1819, and his wife, Amanda C. Boyd, born in Arkansas in 1833, who are the parents of Mary Belle Peer.

Edward Augustus Burton and Mary Belle Peer were the parents of four children, one of whom died in infancy. Of the three who survived to adulthood, two were born in Arkansas, and the last was born in Kansas. These three children were Carrie Charlotte, born Feb. 6, 1880 in Fayetteville, Arkansas, Charles Stephen, born Jan. 3, 1882, in Fayetteville, and Fred Augustus, May 10, 1885 in Green, Sumner County, Kansas.

Carrie Charlotte Burton was the mother of Kathryn Ada Rogers. So much for Kathryn's maternal line, and now on to her father's side of the family, the Rogers.

Edward A. Burton plus a tintype of Mary Belle Peer with her father Edward Peer

Jesse Rogers was probably born about 1770, but that assumption is based on the fact that his marriage took place on Feb. 10, 1795, in Robeson, Pennsylvania, to a woman named Rachel Jackson, who was born in Robeson in 1773. I still have found no record of Jesse's date or place of birth. Rachel's father, grandfather, and great-grandfather were all named Ephraim, and the great-grandfather was the original Jackson family immigrant, having been born in Macclesfield, Cheshire, England in March of 1658, and immigrated to Philadelphia in 1685.

Ephraim Jackson was a member of the Chester Monthly meeting (Quakers), as early as 1687. He married in 1695, Rachel, the daughter of Nicholas Newlin, and purchased land in Edgemont Township. Being a well educated man for his day, he served as a clerk for the Chester Monthly Meeting of Friends, and was employed in much of the civic affairs of the county, for in 1710 he represented it in William Penn's Provincial Assembly. Nicholas Newlin and two of his sons came to America in the early part of 1683 on the ship Liver out of Liverpool. They settled on a large tract of land in Concord Township (now part of Delaware County, Pennsylvania). They transferred from a Quaker meeting in Queen County, Ireland, but, as with most Irish Quakers, their origins seem to be in England.

The name is seen as Newland in early records and claims are made that it originates from the De Newlands, manor lords under the early Norman kings of England. Nicholas Newlin was styled as a yeoman in his will; however during his lifetime he was much more than a small landowner/farmer. He was a member of the Provincial Council of Pennsylvania from 1685-1688; and Justice of the Courts of Chester County 1685-1691. He built and operated a grist mill in Concord Township. The 1694 tax assessment for the Concord Mill was ten pounds. The mill is frame and stone and the miller's house of fieldstone adjoins the mill, and is now as it was originally built, two rooms up and two down, with a beehive oven outside the kitchen fireplace. The mill was purchased in the 1950s by a Newlin descendant, was fully restored, and again grinds corn into meal. The mill and house are listed on the National Historic Register and are operated as a non-profit foundation. The grounds have a blacksmith shop, spring house and log cabin (not part of the original complex). The mill race is stocked with trout and fishing is possible for a fee.

The Newlin Mill Complex in Pennsylvania

Rachel's father, Ephraim Jackson's, will was Proven in October of 1807 and she received a small inheritance, which was probably of help to her, since her husband Jesse Rogers died just a month later, in November of 1807, leaving the widow with six children, ages three to twelve, including five year old twins. All six children were boys. Jesse died without having drawn a will, but we can learn a bit about him from the inventory of his estate. He had two small acreage parcels, one of which was forested land, and he had tools of both the masonry's and the cobbler's trade.

When Jesse's wife Rachel died seven years later, on April 16th, 1814, four of the children were still minors, and the family was then split up. The two sons who were of age, Thomas and William, sold off the property and went their separate ways, while David and Jesse were placed with another family, and the twins, Lot and Evan, were placed with a Mr. Evans and his family.

The twins Evan and Lot remained in Churchtown, Pennsylvania until their deaths. They were masons and carpenters, building numerous homes and public buildings, including a schoolhouse, and were among the workmen who built, in neighboring Lancaster, Pennsylvania, a mansion called Wheatland, which would later become the home of President James Buchanan.

Wheatland, home of President James Buchanan

When I visited Churchtown, PA., a number of years ago, I was in the yard of the Bangor Episcopalian Church, looking at the many gravestones there, many of which are my ancestors. On the corner across the street, a gentleman stood on his front porch watching me for some time, and finally waved me over to his home, introducing himself as the self-appointed town historian and asking which families I was researching. When I told him the Rogers, he gave a wide grin and invited me in to his home to see their work, for the twins were the builders of the original structure. He was able to point out their initial work, and then the additions, made after the Civil War, and again after WWI. The home built by Lot and Evan was about 4,000 square feet, and with the later additions, the home is now 10,000 square feet. The Rogers' built portion was graced with elegant woodwork including 12" crown moldings and an intricate banister, both crafted by hand. Your author descends from Evan, who along with Lot, was born on Oct. 4th, 1802, in Caernarvon Township, Pennsylvania.

Obituary- In Churchtown, Oct 21st Evan ROGERS, in the 52nd year of his age. Apparently in his usual state of health, he closed his store on the night of the 20th inst. At 4 o'clock the next morning his spirit had returned to the god who gave it. So truthful the oft recurring admonition "In the midst of life we are in death." Mr. Rogers had resided in Churchtown upwards of 27 years and there are few men who can number fewer enemies or who are more generally respected for honest worth than the departed. Humble in his pretensions, upright in all his business transactions, cordial in his affections, he has left for his survivors and successors a name without reproach and an example worthy of imitation. A few years since, he connected himself, in communion, with the Presbyterian Church and as a member of that body was consistent and sincere "dying in the confidence of a certain hope" and assurance of a blissful immortality beyond the grave.

C.J.B.Examiner, Independent Whig and Reading Gazette.

Evan married Catherine Carmichael Jenkins, and his twin, Lot, married her older sister, Martha. The Jenkins girls were two of ten children born to David Jenkins and his wife, Mary D. McCamant. The Great-Grandfather of David, also named David (Dafyd), was the original immigrant to the Colonies, from Cardiff, Wales, arriving in Pennsylvania with his wife, Margaret Rees, about 1700. John Jenkins of Windsor, son of the first David, was born 1711, and died at Windsor, 1777. He married about 1730, Rebecca, daughter of David Meredith. (More on the McCamants and Merediths in a moment) John Jenkins settled in 1733, in the Conestoga Valley, in Caernarvon Township, near Churchtown, and was the first settler there. He represented William Branson, an English gentleman, for whom he purchased a large tract of land and erected the Windsor Iron Works, which were among the first in Pennsylvania. The Forge afterwards became the property successively of his son David Jenkins and of his grandson, Robert Jenkins. His wife, Rebecca, died Sept. 5, 1771, aged 64. Both John and Rebecca were buried in the Episcopal Churchyard, Churchtown, Pa. They were members and supporters of that church.

The following is excerpted from the *Jenkins Family Book* by Robert Jenkins, published in 1904:

John Jenkins left a large estate. His sons, John, Isaac and Joseph were made executors of his will, and his "loving friends Jacob Morgan and Robert Armor were therein appointed "overseers of this my will to take care and see it performed according to my true intent and meaning." The will was dated in 1774 and proved May 17, 1777. He devised "that plantation and tract of land whereon I now live" to his son John. He also gave "plantations" to his sons Isaac and Joseph, and money bequests to David, William and Rebecca, also to his granddaughter Mary, the daughter of his son George. He mentions "my kinswoman Annie Rees." Then we get a glimpse of the "peculiar institution" which afterward led to the Civil war, and which then existed in a mild form in Pennsylvania. He says: "Whereas, I have hired my negro man Quash to my son John for eleven years from the first day of March, 1772, at the end of which time I do allow my said negro man to be free from serving any person on my account. And I give my negro woman Cooba to my daughter Rebecca. But if my negro man Quash will be able to pay my daughter the sum of forty pounds at any time within three years after the expiration of the said eleven years, then it is my will that my said negro woman be free, and serve no person any longer than till the said forty pounds are paid." The old Jenkins homestead at Churchtown has been in the family through all succeeding generations, and is now owned by Miss Blanche Nevin, the well-known sculptor, a lineal descendant of said John Jenkins, the first.

And further,

David Jenkins, first son of John and Rebecca (Meredith) Jenkins, born July 2, 1731, married Martha Armor of Pequea, Lancaster Co., died June 2, 1797. He purchased the Windsor Forges and continued to be their proprietor during his life. He was a man of large public spirit and influence. Was Major and perhaps Colonel in the Revolutionary army. "He was very active in organizing opposition to England. Was on the Committee of Safety for the county. In January, 1775, was one of the delegates from his county to a Provincial Convention held in Philadelphia, and also to a convention held there June 18th of the same year. June 25, 1776, he was one of his county's representatives in a conference of delegates from all the counties held in Lancaster. July 4, 1776, he was a
Member of a conference of representatives from the Associators of Pa. In all references to him concerning these conversations he is styled Major. (History of Pa., by Wm. H. Egle, pp. 145, 160, 827, etc.)   His descendants have been numerous, and many of them of much prominence. His son, Robert, received the larger part of the ancestral estates and greatly increased them. Martha (Armor) Jenkins died April 9, 1802. Their children were all born and raised at Windsor.

(Note--- David Jenkins was the Commander of the 10th Battalion of the Pennsylvania Militia 1n 1777. His rank was then Colonel.)

Catherine Carmichael Jenkins' mother, Mary D. McCamant, was the daughter of Isaac McCamant and Rebecca Smith, and the Grand-daughter of Alexander McCamant, born 1674 in Antrim, Ireland, and Mary Black of Scotland. Alexander and Mary emigrated between 1730 and

1735 from County Armagh (County Down) in the north of Ireland, with the second large coming of the Scot-Irish to America. They resided a number of years in Philadelphia, and then located on Pequea Creek, in Lancaster County. In 1733, the land that they took up came from the Penns, by their charter, under their seal and coat of arms. A patent was granted him for these warrants in 1741, as recorded in the land patent office in Harrisburg. A portion of the 300 acres was still in possession of his descendants as late as 1913. Alexander and Mary were the parents of six children, possibly five of which emigrated with them from Ireland. He was a pious Christian and an early member of the Pequea Presbyterian Church, Lancaster County, Pennsylvania, organized in 1724. He died in 1748 leaving a valuable estate. The names of Alexander McCamant, and his son, grandson, and great-grandson, all named Isaac, are memorialized in a stained glass window in the church mentioned above.

Back now for a visit to the Meredith family. Actually, I have very little on this line, but we must begin with it to get to the family of Rush. As noted earlier, Rebecca Meredith was the wife of John Jenkins. The Jenkins were of Welsh ancestry, and the Merediths were as well. Rebecca's father was David Meredith, born in 1675, in Brongwyn, (White Mount), a parish in the county of Cardigan, Wales. He was the initial immigrant into the Pennsylvania Colony for this family. In the traditional naming pattern of the Welsh in that day, his father's name was Meredith ap David, so we know that his father's name was David (Dafyd), but no record is extant for him. Meredith ap David, however is found in Parish registers, and he was also born in Brongwyn, in 1631. Rebecca Meredith's mother, and wife of David Meredith, was Sarah Aurelia Rush. Family legend states that Sarah Aurelia, born in Byberry, Pennsylvania, in 1683, was the first child born to English parents in Philadelphia. (I have been unable to verify this.) William Lucas Rush was the son of John "Old Trooper" Rush, who was a Captain of a troop of horsemen, fighting in Oliver Cromwell's forces, as a separatist in Cromwell's Parliamentary army against the Royalist army of King Charles I of England in the English Civil War of the 1640's. In 1660, Capt. Rush became a Quaker, and in 1682, he moved with his wife, Susannah Lucas, to the colony being established by William Penn. The family lived in Byberry, located about sixteen miles from Philadelphia at the time, which is now a neighborhood in the incorporated city limits. Captain Rush had a number of children, but for our purposes here, I focus on just two of them. One is William Lucas Rush, father of Sarah

113

Aurelia, who married David Meredith, and the other is William's brother, James. James Rush was a gunsmith and farmer in Byberry, and he married Rachel Peart. This couple had several children as well, and one was a son named John, who married Susannah Harvey; another group of children ensued, including Dr. Benjamin Rush, whose signature on the Declaration of Independence, can be found just under that fine flourish of John Hancock. Dr. Rush was the Surgeon General for George Washington's Continental Army, and the founder of Dickenson Collage in Carlisle, Pennsylvania. He also served at the University of Pennsylvania as a Professor of Chemistry, Medical Theory, and Clinical Practice. The Rush Medical College in Chicago is named in his honor. The common ancestor for Benjamin Rush and Sarah Aurelia Rush, is her grandfather, the Old Trooper, John, which makes Sarah and Benjamin first cousins, one generation removed.

With apologies for the necessary side-trips to the associated family lines, I will return now to Evan Rogers and his wife, Catherine Carmichael Jenkins, in Churchtown, PA. To this union were born four sons and two daughters; first were twins, Jesse and Mary in December of 1835, both of whom died young; Jesse at three, and Mary at fifteen. Next was David Linford , born January 8th, 1837 and died, unmarried, May 21st, 1899, in El Paso, Illinois. Next, on May 3rd, 1842, was my Great-Grandfather, Thornton Lot Rogers, followed by Martha Francis "Fanny" in November of 1843, and James M., in June of 1850.

Thornton Lot Rogers completed his schooling and by the 1860 census record, we find the eighteen year old living in the home of a physician, Robert Bunn, in Ebensville, PA., where he is serving as a clerk. Ten years later, in the 1870 census, Thornton is found in El Paso, a booming small town in Woodford County, Illinois. With him are an infant son, George, and a young wife, Cynthia Elizabeth (Fridley) Rogers. George is the first of five children born to the couple, and is the only one born in Illinois.

A moment here on the Fridley family, and then back for the remainder of Thornton's brood. George Fridley was born about 1814 in the Finger Lakes region of New York, and in 1838 he accompanied his cousin, Harriet (Fridley) Fenner, and her husband, Felix Fenner, to Tazewell County, Illinois, and the town of Tremont. George was working as a cabinetmaker there, but had left behind his favorite girl in Elmira, New York, and in 1840, he returned to marry her. In the Elmira Republican, Elmira Gazette, Elmira NY newspaper was this notice:

> Married by the Rev. Benj. Shipman on the 6th inst, (Feb 6, 1840) Mr. George Fridley of Tremont IL to Miss Eliza M. Baldwin of Elmira.

After the wedding George and Eliza Marie then moved back to Tremont, where their first child, Willy, was born, in 1843, but died and was buried in Tremont just three years later. On February 28, 1845, a second child was born, a daughter, Cynthia Elizabeth, who would wed Thornton Rogers. Not long after Willie's death the family moved to the town of Peoria, and the 1850 census of that place lists George as a cabinetmaker. By the 1860 census, George is listed as a Grocer. Three more children were born to the couple, being Elizabeth Marie in 1847, Fanny B., in 1849, and George in January of 1850. George Jr., and his mother died during childbirth, and the mother was returned to Tremont, where she was buried along side her beloved first born, Willy.

Soon after, George remarried, to Amanda Harl. They had three daughters, of whom the first two died in their first year, with only the third, Mary, surviving to adulthood.

Thornton Lot and Cynthia Elizabeth Rogers moved after 1870 to Sedgewick County, Kansas, and appear on the 1875 Kansas State census in Attica Township. The next record is the 1880 federal census for Kansas, and as far as genealogical research goes, it is the most unsettling record I have had to deal with. The following is the information given for the first *three households* on page eleven:

1. Rodgers, Thornton L.   male   age 39 Married Farmer
  ------------- Sintha [Cynthia] female   age 34 Married Keeping house
  ------------- George son   male   age 10
  ------------- Rosena daughter female age 5
  ------------- Katie   daughter female age 5/12

2. Rodgers, Lizzie   female   age 33 Married Keeping house
  -------------- Pearl   daughter female   age 7
  --------------- Fridley son   male   age 5

3. Rodgers, James   male   age 30 Bachelor Farmer
   Rodgers, Ralph   male   age 35 Married Farmer

Well, OK, this looks at least, fairly straight forward, but there are some problems to deal with now. Family number one is definitely the correct family for Thornton, but the problem is the five year old daughter, Rosena. She never appears again in any record; moreover, the child who should be listed as a five year old son is Rodney Fridley Rogers, my Grandfather. Rodney does show up in the 1885 state census as a ten year old son, and there is no Rosena there. Family number two, Lizzie, is Eliza Marie (Fridley) Rogers, Cynthia's younger sister, who is married, but estranged from, Ralph Rogers, shown in family number three. Ralph, Lizzie, and two year old Pearl, were shown together on the 1875 state census. James Rogers, the bachelor shown in family number three is Thornton's younger brother. So, the question looms, where is Rodney, and what became of Rosena? The Rosena part of the answer, I believe, was provided by my mother, when she told me once that there was a child buried on the farm, down by the creek, but there was no marker on the grave, and she did not know who it was. I firmly believe that it was Rosena. Rest in Peace, little one. In the 1885 state census, Lizzie, Ralph, and Pearl are not listed.

The entire federal census of 1890, to the chagrin of genealogists everywhere, was regrettably lost to a fire, and as of the 1895 state record, Thornton is deceased, and Cynthia, Rodney, Katherine, and a younger brother, Samuel, are all that are left at home. The eldest son George has moved out on his own. Also, in 1895, Lizzie, Pearl, and a younger sister, Mary, are living in town (Wichita), and there is still no Ralph in the household. My first reaction to all this was a bit plaintive, for I wondered if, since Thornton had lost a son, and Lizzie was raising children without a father in the house, could it be possible that Lizzie's five year old, Fridley, of 1880, had become Thornton's ten year old, Rodney Fridley, of 1885. It would make sense for Thornton to take the boy, to ease the burden on his sister-in-law. But, since the gods that hover over the shoulder of genealogists enjoy throwing curve balls, I find that that younger sister, Mary, daughter of Lizzie, was born in Colorado. So, the search goes on, and behold, the marital relationship between Ralph and Lizzie turns out to be, an on-again, off-again, type of relationship. And to my chagrin, I find Ralph, and his son, Fridley, living in Colorado. So, in the end, it comes down to the all too common answer found in this type of research---the census taker who listed Rosena, simply failed to list Rodney (quite possibly Rosena's twin brother) in the home of

Thornton and Cynthia in that perplexing 1880 census. You, dear reader, may have struck upon one final question in all of this; who is Ralph? Well, even though the last name is the same, I can find no actual relationship between these Rogers families. Thornton, and two generations further back (Evan and Jesse), are all Pennsylvanians, whereas Ralph was born in Illinois, of a father from Virginia. The cousin relationship may exist, but I have found no such link. Ralph is just a brother-in-law to Thornton due to Cynthia and Lizzie being sisters.

The children of Thornton and Cynthia have been introduced, so now I take up one of them, my grandfather, **Rodney Fridley Rogers**. Rodney Rogers was born August 19th, 1875, when Ulysses S. Grant was the President, and only thirty-seven stars were emblazoned on the American Flag. The Battle of the Little Big Horn was still a year away. Rodney was born, lived, and died on the farmland that his father had settled on.

He was just a simple farmer, and yet, in many ways, he was a remarkable man. Rodney was just sixteen when his father died, and with his older brother, George, already away from home studying law, the day to day operations of the farm fell onto the teenager's shoulders. Until the year prior, Thornton, George, and Rodney had worked the 160 acres of the farm as a team, but now, with the spring planting season approaching, Rodney faced the task of preparing the soil on his own, using a plow and team of horses.. He bent his back to the test, for he needed to support his mother, a twelve year old sister, Katherine, and a six year old brother, Sam. The responsibilities of adulthood came very early for Rodney.

The Rogers farm had a stream that ran through it, and as the Kansas summer sun shed its heat, the stream would begin to dry up. Long before there was any "environmental movement", Rodney knew how to shepherd the farm's resources, so as the summer approached, he would take buckets and a net to the stream, where he would dip out the fish, and carry them in the buckets back to the farmyard, and there deposit them into the large round tank that held water for his horses. In late autumn, when the stream was revived, he would reverse the process and return the fish to their home waters.

In 1918, the world was struck with an influenza pandemic, commonly called today, the Great Spanish Flu, in which an estimated thirty to fifty million people worldwide perished. Nearly every one of Rodney's neighbors were sick, and Christmas was just a couple of weeks away.

Rodney, and his daughter, Kathryn (my mom), were the only two people on the Attica Township farms, who were not ill. They took it upon themselves to take their 1916 Ford Model T, tin lizzie, into Wichita to do the gift shopping for all their neighbors. While they were shopping, snow began to fall, and by the time that they were making the return trip, the snowfall had increased to near blizzard conditions, and, about a mile from home, the car slid off the road and into a ditch. Rodney and Kathryn were forced to abandon the car and make their way home on foot. Over the next few days, they recovered the gifts from the stranded auto and delivered them to the neighbors by a horse drawn wagon. The tin lizzie remained in the ditch for several months until the spring thaws released it.

On February 20th, 1907, Rodney Fridley Rogers took a bride, one Carrie Charlotte Burton, whose ancestry was detailed in the early pages of this chapter. To this couple was born first, on October 2nd, 1908, my mother, Kathryn Ada Rogers. Next, a son, Walter Burton Rogers, on July 11th, 1911. Walter was afflicted with Scarlet Fever as a child, leaving him with a poor heart, and in the fall of 1929, he was kicked in the chest by a horse. He never recovered from that injury, and on December 1st, he passed away. The third child born to the Rogers was Dorothy Helen, on August 20th, 1915, and she lived a long life, passing away from natural causes on October 27th, 2007. The final child born to the family was named Carma, born October 27th, 1920, but lived only a little over two weeks.

Rodney and Carrie Rogers ca.1955

Thus ends the ancestral trail of Kathryn Ada Rogers, the second wife of David Cleborn McNair (see chapter six).

Afterword

Some personal observations are in order here. The work that culminated in this book spanned over three decades and I must say that this was some of the most enjoyable time in my life. To coin a word, it felt "Sherlockian." There was no "google" back then; no ancestry dot com; indeed, no internet. Thus I went to libraries, to historical societies, to churchyards and cow pastures that held headstones, and made innumerable phone calls and mail requests for copies of birth and death certificates, along with will and probate records.

However, as mentioned in the introduction to this book, I was just gathering names, dates, and places; the real search for our ancestor's histories began in the second half of those three decades. With greater access to census, pension, church, and military records, along with newspapers and books online, I was able to begin to piece together the travels, work, ambitions and motives that fueled their daily lives.

One item of note is the relative longevity of our ancestors. Daniel of chapter one lived into his seventies and quite possibly his eighties. Coming forward, James was nearly seventy and his son John lived to sixty-nine as well. James Claiborne lived through the Mexican War and suffered great hardships for himself and family during the Civil War, and yet lived to the ripe old age of eighty-four. His son, David Bruce, lived to ninety-two and his wife Sarah Elizabeth Kester (granny Mac to me) also reached ninety-two. Of course some died at younger ages; Sarah Elizabeth's father died at age forty-three, but that was after riding his horse through an icy river during a bear hunt, which most of us today would likely avoid, although I would not rule out my nephew Adrian aka Maverick! Solomon Prewitt Sr. died in 1852 but not before reaching 110, while Boniface Burton of chapter eight died in 1669 at 113 years. The lesson to be learned here is that average life expectancy (world) at birth has been low over the years, such as thirty-one in 1900, forty-eight in 1950, and in 2010 it was sixty-seven. The key to this is the word "average". Child mortality was so much greater in the past, and so the "average" age was much lower, but now modern medicine is bringing the average up nicely. So McNairs, live long and prosper! Oh, and don't forget to feed your IRA --- you are going to need it one day.

Another observation can be made about our ancestry and that is about our national origins. We McNairs certainly think of ourselves as Scots or at the very least Scot-Irish but of course that is pretty much simply because of our last name. We would do well to remember that string of fine women who have shared our journey through time; the Welsh Martha Price; the German MaryAnn Scherertz; the Welsh Harriet Manes; the English Susan Patsy Fields. Kester may well be a German name, while the Eights were definitely from the Netherlands. The Burtons were English and the Jenkins were Welsh. The Peer family was very likely French. So just how Scot are we really? I had a DNA sample taken and I can report that I am ninety-nine-point-seven percent European, but that remaining little bit includes West African and even Sardinian. Included in my European roots are Scandinavian bits (My Vikings of chapter eight) and even a shade over three percent Neanderthal!

Of course the mixing doesn't end there either but continues on. My Brother Michael's second wife has Croatian roots and his daughter-in-law is of Cuban extraction. My son Shannon married a lovely lady from Japan. I can only say keep the kilts well mended and wear them proudly but let us not forget to give a nod and a smile to those other flags occasionally.

If I could now have one wish it would be for a time machine. What a thrill it would be to simply knock on Daniel's door and introduce myself as his fourth-great-grandson. Oh what questions I would have for him. When and where were you born kind sir? Who were your parents; your grandparents; where were they from? The same questions would need to be asked of Jesse Rogers, my third-great-grandfather on my mother's side. These questions reveal the failings of this book, that being that I have so many unanswered questions. Fortunately though, that opens the door for future family historians to find those answers and share them with the family as I have attempted to do. Those answers are out there somewhere in church records, parish and county records, family bibles, and more, just waiting for you to go and find them. And please, please, if I am still living, share them with me too. If I'm dead, for Pete's sake, invent that time machine and come find me! The time machine we have right now is called history for it is a one-way machine that only allows us to look backward, but imagine if we could make it a two-way machine that would allow Daniel and Jesse and all the rest of the fine folks herein to come forward in time and see what their loins have wrought! Would they be amazed and proud of all of us, or might they find a hearty laugh in their bellies and let it loose on us? I can only pray that one day we can all meet that way and share in the pride and the laughter.

I hope that this book has been helpful to those who would wish to know the history of the families that have led the way to "us", and might hopefully be a springboard for future generations to continue these stories.

In the event you wish to contact me with corrections or comments, my e-mail address is: rogerbmcnair@gmail.com

NOTES

NOTES

NOTES